The Decision Principles

*Conquering Decision-Making
Obstacles in Life and Business*

Rich Bello

AROOTAH

ISBN: 9798392845286

About The Author

RICH BELLO

Chairman and Chief Executive Officer, Arootah

Co-Founder, Chief Operating Officer, Blue Ridge Capital

Rich Bello is the chairman and CEO of Arootah, an organization that specializes in empowering leaders with peak performance strategies that unlock their potential in their personal and professional lives.

Rich has a deep-rooted passion for both personal and professional development. Rich and the Arootah team empower clients to reach their highest potential. He helps clients achieve maximum results by setting clear objectives and designing strategic plans with accountability strategies for execution.

Before Arootah, Rich served as co-founder and chief operating officer of Blue Ridge Capital, a firm with approximately $10 billion in assets under management at its peak. Prior to his 25 years at Blue Ridge, Rich held senior positions at Ernst and Young, Tiger Management, and Morgan Stanley. He studied at The Wharton School of the University of Pennsylvania.

Amongst his various philanthropic endeavors, Rich founded and proudly serves on the iMentor Advisory Board of Directors. This organization has mentored more than 36,000 high school and college students, most of whom are from low-income communities.

Acknowledgments

I would like to especially acknowledge the coaches who have lovingly guided and awakened the spirit within me. Their patience, wisdom, compassion, and tough love carried me through the challenges in my life and inspired me to reach for more.

My gratitude goes out to my colleagues at Blue Ridge Capital for providing me with an amazing opportunity to hone the craft I love — personal and professional growth and business excellence. You always kept our standards at the highest levels.

I want to express my sincere appreciation to the Arootah team for the perseverance and teamwork it took to complete this book and their tireless efforts to see our mission through.

Finally, I would like to thank my family for lovingly putting up with me always and especially as I beta-test The Principles on you. I love you all.

Table of Contents

Introduction

*"The quality of our decision-making processes
directly correlates with the level of success and
fulfillment we experience in the realms of our
personal lives, careers, and businesses."*

— *Rich Bello*

As someone who is dedicating their life to studying and teaching peak performance in the personal, career, and business realms, I often find myself asking a critical question:

*Why don't we <u>always</u> do what is in our best
interests?*

Despite our best intentions, we sometimes make seemingly illogical choices that lead to negative consequences. In fact, as I'm writing this introduction, I'm craving a cookie as I write. Mind you. I fashion myself to be a "health coach." In my defense, the cookie is advertised by its packaging as a "healthy" cookie (No sugar. Grain Free. Organic. Etc. Etc.). But let's face it; it's a cookie! Without even digging deep into the ingredients, I know it is unhealthy, and a logical decision would dictate that I let go of this urge and not eat it. But I'm pretty sure that I am going to eat it anyway. Why? Read on.

In my journey to understand this phenomenon, I've realized that effective decision-making lies at the heart of achieving success in the three realms: personal, career, and business. Efficient and effective decision-making should be the foundation upon which we build our lives, careers, and businesses and it is the key to attaining positive outcomes. As a coach of leaders and a leader of coaches, this crucial skill is of the utmost importance.

The key to success in the field of decision-making, or any field for that matter, lies not just in mastering the subject matter but also in creating efficient and effective processes to apply that knowledge. I take great pride in my ability to distill complex ideas into simple, easy-to-understand processes that can be easily digested and applied. This "conversion process" is not only crucial for mastering a subject but also for teaching it effectively to others.

Simply acquiring knowledge is not enough - we must also apply it in practical ways. Knowledge will not apply itself. That's why I believe in creating and leveraging technology to help streamline and enhance the decision-making process. Ultimately, it is the combination of accumulating knowledge, following a systematic process, and leveraging technological innovation that leads to true mastery and success in decision-making.

In today's fast-paced world, making effective decisions is more critical than ever before. Leaders face complex and challenging decision-making scenarios every day. The ability to navigate these challenges and make informed choices can be the difference between success and failure.

However, decision-making is not always straightforward. Various factors, including emotions, cognitive biases, analysis paralysis, and group dynamics can influence it. These obstacles can make it difficult for leaders to make rational, informed, and unbiased decisions.

In this book, "The Decision Principles: Conquering Decision-Making Obstacles in Life, Career, and Business," I aim to provide leaders with practical strategies to overcome common decision-making challenges. I present 12 key Principles for leaders to develop a more robust decision-making process and achieve more successful outcomes.

From mastering the art and science of decision-making to defeating indecision caused by analysis paralysis, decision fatigue, and information overload. Each chapter in this book explores a specific decision-making obstacle and provides guidance on how to overcome it.

We address how to balance logic and intuition, cultivate positive habits, collaborate for consensus, and make strategic decisions that have positive downstream effects on other decisions.

The principles for making personal, career, and business decisions are largely the same. They apply equally to both individual and team decision-making.

Through our exploration of these key principles, I aim to equip leaders with the tools and knowledge they need to make informed decisions. By applying these principles, we believe leaders can overcome common obstacles, avoid pitfalls, and achieve greater success in all aspects of life.

Through critical thinking, self-reflection, and practical strategies, readers will learn to improve their decision-making processes, leading to greater success and fulfillment in all realms of life, career, and business. Enjoy.

10 The Decision Principles

We address how to balance logic and intuition, cultivate positive habits, collaborate for consensus, and make strategic decisions that have positive downstream effects on other decisions.

The principles for making personal, career, and business decisions are largely the same. They apply equally to both individual and team decision-making.

Through our exploration of these key principles, I aim to equip leaders with the tools and knowledge they need to make informed decisions. By applying these principles, we believe leaders can overcome common obstacles, avoid pitfalls, and achieve greater success in all aspects of life.

Through critical thinking, self-reflection, and practical strategies, readers will learn to improve their decision-making processes, leading to greater success and fulfillment in all realms of life, career, and business. Enjoy.

Principle 1

Master the Art and Science of Decision-Making

"It takes 20 years to build a reputation and five minutes to ruin it. If you think about that, you'll do things differently." — Warren Buffett

Unlocking the Keys to Success in Life, Career, and Business

Mastering the art and science of decision-making involves analyzing information, evaluating options, and selecting the best course of action to achieve desired goals. The ability to make decisions is a crucial skill that helps you make informed choices that align with your personal values. By developing effective decision-making skills, you can reduce errors, boost confidence, and increase your chances of success in all aspects of life and business.

Key Question
Why is mastering the skill of decision-making a worthy investment of our time?

Have you ever made a decision that you regretted for days, weeks, or even years? Of course, you have — and so have I. Warren Buffett's quotation here drives the point home well in that he is clearly referring to a poor *decision* that has been made quickly that destroyed a reputation that took an entire lifetime to build.

We all make bad decisions, even those of us who study and write books about decision-making. This is understandable, especially when you consider the sheer number of decisions we make daily, which some sources suggest is a staggering 35,000![1] As I was writing this book, my editor suggested that I provide a personal anecdote of a poor decision I had made. Being that I intended this book to be the definitive guide on decision-making, I told her that I didn't think it was a good idea because "I don't want my readers to lose confidence in me." She responded, "Well, that's a bad decision right there." And she was absolutely correct — for all the reasons you're probably thinking. So let me tell you about another bad decision I made.

> *I was working with my first executive coach very early in my career and practicing risk/reward challenges. Taking risks involves building up a high level of courage, so I was finding all kinds of ways to practice courage. On one occasion, I decided to kill two birds with one stone by going for a long run in Central Park — after midnight. I figured I would get some great exercise while practicing courage. I laced up my sneakers and set off on my run, feeling invincible and fearless. I decided not only to run in the park but to run in the more "dangerous" areas of the park. And that's what I did. The next day I was excited to tell my coach how "courageous" I had been last night, and when I told him about my bravery, he said, "Rich, that's not called 'courage.'" I was excited! I figured he had some advanced coaching terms like "Super Brave." I asked curiously, "Really? What's it called then?" He said, "That's called 'stupid!' Don't do that again." He was right. Had I known how to correctly analyze and assess my options, I would have made a better, and in this case, safer, decision.*

Common Poor Decisions

Here are a few examples of poor decisions commonly made in the personal, career, and business realms that caused unnecessary pain and suffering that could have been avoided

---

[1] Krockow, E.M. (2018, September 27). How many decisions do we make each day? *Psychology Today.*
https://www.psychologytoday.com/us/blog/stretching-theory/201809/how-many-decisions-do-we-make-each-day

had they trained for and applied the crucial skill of making quality decisions.

Common Poor *Personal* Decisions

1. **Choosing the wrong partner/spouse.** This decision can lead to emotional pain, divorce, and financial loss.
2. **Failing to prioritize self-care and personal well-being.** This decision can lead to physical and mental health problems, burnout, and decreased quality of life.
3. **Making impulsive financial decisions.** This decision can lead to debt, financial stress, and instability.
4. **Failing to set boundaries with toxic people.** This decision can lead to emotional abuse, manipulation, and codependency.
5. **Making decisions based on fear or societal expectations rather than personal values and goals.** This decision can lead to feelings of regret, lack of fulfillment, and a sense of living someone else's life.

Common Poor *Career* Decisions

1. **Staying in a job that is unfulfilling or toxic.** This decision can lead to burnout, stress, and a lack of career growth.
2. **Failing to negotiate salary or promotions.** This decision can lead to missed opportunities and financial loss.
3. **Choosing a career path based on societal expectations rather than personal interests or passions.** This decision can lead to a lack of fulfillment and regret.
4. **Failing to develop necessary skills or pursue professional development.** This decision can lead to stagnation and a lack of career advancement.
5. **Making career decisions based solely on financial gain rather than personal fulfillment or alignment with values.** This decision can lead to a lack of meaning and purpose in work.

Common Poor *Business* Decisions

1. **Ignoring customer feedback and concerns.** This decision can lead to decreased customer loyalty, decreased sales, and a negative brand reputation.

2. **Failing to adapt to changing market conditions or technological advancements.** This decision can lead to a decreased market share and loss of competitiveness.

3. **Making unethical or illegal decisions.** This decision can lead to legal action, fines, and damage to the brand's reputation.

4. **Neglecting employee well-being and development.** This decision can lead to high turnover rates, decreased productivity, and decreased employee morale.

5. **Making decisions based solely on short-term gains rather than long-term sustainability and growth.** This decision can lead to decreased profitability and instability in the long run.

Food for thought: According to a report by the Project Management Institute, organizations lose an average of $109 million for every $1 billion spent on projects due to poor decision-making.[2]

The negative outcomes of these decisions can be avoided if you have the knowledge and skill to make better choices, as well as a structured process with which to use that knowledge. Without the guidance of a sound decision-making process, you may miss out on the chance to attain personal fulfillment, career growth, and business success, highlighting the importance of possessing

---

[2]Project Management Institute. (2018). Pulse of the Profession. https://www.pmi.org/learning/thought-leadership/pulse/pulse-of-the-profession-2018

effective strategies to avoid the negative consequences that result from poor choices.

Categories of Decisions

We make a wide range of decisions every day, from what to eat for breakfast to what career path to pursue. It is wise to analyze these decisions in a classified fashion as many hold similar characteristics in how we make them. These decisions can be categorized in different ways depending on the factors that influence them and the context in which they are made. In this section, we will explore and define some of the most common types of decisions that we make and some examples of each.

Routine Decisions

- Made frequently
- Not much, if any, thought or deliberation
- *Examples:* Deciding what to wear or deciding what to eat for breakfast

Strategic Decisions

- Involve planning
- Weigh different options to achieve a specific goal
- *Examples:* Deciding on a career path, selecting a college major, or developing a business strategy

Ethical Decisions

- Choosing between right and wrong
- Involve ethical considerations
- *Examples:* Deciding whether to report a coworker's unethical behavior or deciding whether to donate money to a charitable cause

Emotional Decisions

- Influenced by feelings and emotions
- Lack of rational thought

- *Examples:* Deciding to end a relationship based on feelings of anger or making an impulsive purchase because of a strong emotional response

Group Decisions

- Made by groups of people
- *Examples:* Deciding on a course of action in a team meeting or deciding on a family vacation destination through discussion and compromise

Financial Decisions

- Involve money and financial resources
- *Examples:* Deciding whether to invest in a particular stock or deciding how to save for retirement

Personal Decisions

- Relate to one's personal life
- Involve different options
- *Examples:* Deciding whether to have children, where to live, which hobbies to take up

Organizational Decisions

- Made within organizations, such as businesses and non-profits
- Weigh the need of multiple stakeholders
- *Examples:* Deciding to launch a new product or deciding how to allocate resources among different departments

Risky Decisions

- Options have uncertain outcomes
- Require balancing potential risks with potential rewards
- *Examples:* Deciding whether to invest in a high-risk stock, whether to undergo an experimental medical procedure

Consumer Decisions

- Relate to the purchasing of goods and services
- Compare different products or brands on features, price, or other factors
- *Examples:* Deciding which smartphone to buy or which hotel to stay at during a vacation

Conclusion

Mastering the skill of decision-making is a worthy investment of your time because it empowers you to make informed choices and align your decisions with your personal values, which can lead to greater success and fulfillment in all aspects of your life and business. This chapter highlighted the importance of developing effective decision-making skills and presented examples of poor personal, career, and business decisions that could have been avoided with better decision-making strategies. By understanding the different factors that influence our ability to make decisions and learning to use structured decision-making processes, we can make better choices and achieve greater success and fulfillment. So, investing in your decision-making skills can significantly improve your life, career, and business.

Summary

1. Effective decision-making is crucial for individuals, careers, and businesses.

2. Poor decisions can cause unnecessary pain and suffering individuals could have avoided with effective decision-making.

3. The five common personal decisions that can cause significant pain and suffering include choosing the wrong partner, failing to prioritize self-care, making impulsive financial decisions, failing to set boundaries with toxic people, and making decisions based on fear or societal expectations.

4. The five common career decisions that can cause significant pain and suffering include: staying in an unfulfilling job, failing to negotiate salary or promotions, choosing a career path based on societal expectations, failing to develop necessary skills to improve performance, and making career decisions based solely on financial gain.

5. The five common business decisions that can cause significant pain and suffering include: ignoring customer feedback, failing to adapt to changing market conditions, making unethical or illegal decisions, neglecting employee well-being and development, and making decisions based solely on short-term gains.

6. Decisions can be categorized into routine decisions, strategic decisions, ethical decisions, financial decisions, operational decisions, organizational decisions, and interpersonal decisions.

7. Routine decisions are made frequently and often without much thought or deliberation, such as what to wear or what to eat for breakfast.

8. Strategic decisions involve planning and weighing different options to achieve a specific goal, such as selecting a college major or developing a business strategy.

9. Ethical decisions involve choosing between right and wrong and often involve moral or ethical considerations, such as whether to report a coworker's unethical behavior or donate money to a charitable cause.

10. Effective decision-making involves applying knowledge and skills to a structured process to make better choices.

20 The Decision Principles

1. Why is effective decision-making important for individuals and businesses?

    It helps individuals achieve goals and avoid negative consequences.

2. What are some common personal decisions that can cause significant pain and suffering?

    Relationships, health, finances, and lifestyle choices.

3. What are some common career decisions that can cause significant pain and suffering?

    Choosing a career path, leaving a job, and pursuing an education.

4. What are some common business decisions that can cause significant pain and suffering?

    Mergers and acquisitions, layoffs, investments, and product development.

5. How can decisions be categorized?

    Routine, strategic, and ethical in their importance.

6. What are routine decisions?

    Decisions that are made regularly and do not require significant consideration or analysis.

7. What are strategic decisions?

    Decisions with a long-term perspective and have an impact.

8. What are ethical decisions?

    Decisions that involve moral principles and values.

9. What is involved in effective decision-making?

    Analyzing relevant information, considering consequences.

10. How can individuals, careers, and businesses benefit from effective decision-making?

    Achieving their goals, avoiding negative consequences, improving outcomes, and building a positive reputation.

Exercises

1. Reflect on a personal decision you regret and consider what could have been done differently to make a better decision.

2. Identify a career decision you made based on societal expectations rather than personal interests or passions, and reflect on how this decision has affected your career.

3. Think of a business decision a company made based solely on short-term gains rather than long-term sustainability and growth and analyze the consequences of this decision.

4. Categorize the choices you made today into routine, strategic, ethical, financial, operational, organizational, or interpersonal decisions.

5. Practice making a decision using a structured process, such as identifying the problem, generating options, evaluating alternatives, and choosing the best solution.

6. Read a case study about a business that made a poor decision and analyze what went wrong and what could have been done differently.

7. Interview a successful individual or business owner about their decision-making process and strategies.

8. Write a list of your values and goals and use them to guide your decision-making in your personal and professional life.

9. Evaluate the consequences of a recent decision and consider what could have been done differently to achieve the desired outcome.

10. Brainstorm ways your company or organization could improve its decision-making process to avoid poor decisions and promote better outcomes.

22 The Decision Principles

Principle 2

Expose Cognitive Biases

*"Few people are capable of expressing with
equanimity opinions that differ from the prejudices
of their social environment. Most people are even
incapable of forming such opinions."*

- Albert Einstein

Uncovering the Hidden Flaws of the Mind for Better Judgments

Exposing cognitive biases involves identifying and acknowledging biases, such as confirmation bias and availability bias, that can affect decision making. By recognizing these biases, you can make more objective and rational decisions and avoid being unduly influenced by subjective factors. This process is crucial for optimal decision making because biases can lead to subpar — and even irrational — decisions that can have negative consequences. By making informed and objective decisions based on facts and evidence, you can increase your chances of success.

---

*Key Question
How do we become aware of and therefore
interrupt cognitive biases in order to make better
decisions?*

In the quotation above, Albert Einstein underscores the gravity of recognizing and overcoming one of the strongest obstacles to making informed and rational decisions: **cognitive biases**. Cognitive biases are inherent flaws in the way we process information and make judgments; these flaws, in turn, can lead to errors in decision-making. Recognizing and overcoming cognitive biases is crucial for making quality decisions.

Why Do We Have Cognitive Biases?

Is this some cruel hoax by the Great Architect? Why wouldn't our brains' cognitive abilities be designed to help us make complex decisions instead of hindering our decision-making process?

Cognitive biases are not deliberate or malicious tricks played on us by some higher power. Rather, they are a product of the way the brain has evolved to process massive amounts of information and make decisions in the face of incomplete or ambiguous data. In other words, cognitive biases are, in fact, designed to *assist* our cognitive decision-making processes — and they do, just not for decisions that require more deliberate thinking, as we will investigate when we example Principle 3, which discusses this type of thinking.

In his book *Behave*, Robert Sapolsky notes that cognitive biases can be seen as "byproducts of adaptations." Our brains have evolved to process vast amounts of information and make rapid decisions based on incomplete or uncertain data, often in high-stakes situations. Thus, our brains have developed a variety of cognitive shortcuts, or heuristics, that allow us to process information quickly and efficiently, even if that means relying on flawed or incomplete data. This efficiency works well when we need to make rapid decisions with limited options, like when a sabretooth tiger is chasing us; it doesn't work as well when we need to make more complex decisions and have the time to deliberate.

For example, the negativity bias is a cognitive bias that refers to our very human tendency to give more weight and attention to negative experiences, information, or stimuli than positive experiences, information, or stimuli. This bias may have served an evolutionary purpose by helping our ancestors avoid danger and survive in their environments so that if someone hears rustling in the bushes, for example, they immediately assume it's a predator lurking nearby rather than assuming it's just the wind. While this bias can sometimes lead us to experience irrational fears or anxieties, it can also help us stay alert and prepared in potentially dangerous situations.

Daniel Kahneman similarly argues that cognitive biases are a natural consequence of the way our brains are wired to process information. Our brains rely on automatic, intuitive thinking to process intel and make decisions quickly and efficiently. However, this type of thinking is also prone to errors and biases, particularly in situations where we may not have all the relevant information or wherein which our emotions are highly engaged. We will examine this more thoroughly in Principle 3.

Cognitive biases can have serious detrimental effects in certain situations. For example, a 2018 journal article reports that cognitive biases can impact clinical decision-making in healthcare, leading to misdiagnosis and inappropriate treatment.[3]

Overall, cognitive biases can be seen as a natural consequence of the way our brains have evolved to process information and make decisions. While they can lead us to make errors and mistakes in judgment, they are also a necessary component of our ability to navigate the complex and often uncertain world around us. It is important to be aware of these biases and consciously evaluate our thinking processes to make the best decisions possible. Likewise, it is important to recognize that our brains are not perfect decision-making machines and that cognitive biases are a natural part of the human experience that must be taken into account.

---

[3] O'Sullivan, E. D., & Schofield, S. J. (2018). Cognitive bias in clinical medicine. *The Journal of the Royal College of Physicians of Edinburgh*, *48*(3), 225–232.

What Are the Top Cognitive Biases That Affect Decision-Making?

Below are some of the most common cognitive biases that have the potential to negatively impact the process of making decisions.

1. **Confirmation Bias.** The inclination to search for, interpret, and recall information in a way that confirms one's pre-existing beliefs or hypotheses while giving disproportionately less consideration to alternative possibilities.

   Example: A person who believes that a particular stock will perform well may only seek out news articles and expert opinions that support their belief about a company's potential growth while ignoring or dismissing any contradictory information (*e.g.*, declining sales).

2. **Overconfidence Bias.** The tendency to overestimate one's abilities, knowledge, and/or the accuracy of one's beliefs and predictions.

   Example: An investor who is convinced that a particular stock will perform well may invest a large sum of money into it, despite not having thoroughly researched the company or its financials.

   Fast Fact: A study by McKinsey & Company found that managers who are overconfident in their abilities are more likely to make poor decisions and experience lower performance outcomes.[4]

---

[4] Johnson, D., Fowler, J. (2011). The evolution of overconfidence. *Nature* 477, 317–320.

3. **Availability Bias.** The disposition to overestimate the importance or likelihood of events based on how easily they come to mind, often due to recent or vivid experiences, and/or how readily available that information is.

   Example: An investor who avoids investing in airline stocks after a recent plane crash, despite statistical evidence that such incidents are rare and do not necessarily impact the industry's overall performance.

4. **Anchoring Bias.** The propensity to rely too heavily on the first piece of information encountered when making decisions, even if it is not necessarily relevant or accurate.

   Example: An investor who decides to buy a stock based solely on its current price without considering any other factors that may impact its future performance.

5. **Hindsight Bias.** The susceptibility to see past events as more predictable than they were after the fact.

   Example: An investor who claims that they knew a particular stock was going to decline in value, despite not having taken any action to sell it beforehand.

6. **Framing Effect.** The tendency for people to react differently to the same information depending on how it is presented (or the way in which information is presented can impact the way in which people perceive and make decisions about it).

   Example: An investor who is more likely to invest in a stock that is presented as having a "60% chance of success" rather than one that is presented as having a "40% chance of failure," even though the two statements convey the same information.

7. **Group Bias.** The proclivity to favor or identify with members of one's own group, often at the expense of those outside the group.

    Example: A business owner who only hires employees from their own social or professional network rather than seeking out qualified candidates from diverse backgrounds.

8. **Halo Effect.** This is a cognitive bias where people's overall impression of a person influences their perception of that person's individual traits.

    Example: In a study by Nisbett and Wilson (1977), participants tasted several wines and rated them on various qualities. They were then told that two of the wines were actually the same, but one was labeled as more expensive. Participants consistently rated the "more expensive" wine as superior, even though they were identical to the cheaper wine.[5]

9. **Sunk Cost Fallacy.** The tendency to continue investing time, money, or other resources into a project or decision even when it is no longer rational to do so, based on the belief that previous investments necessitate further investment.

    Example: A business owner who continues to pour money into a failing venture because they have already invested significant time and money into it, rather than cutting their losses and pursuing other opportunities.

---

[5] Nisbett RE, Wilson TD. (1977). Telling more than we can know: Verbal reports on mental process. Psychological Review, 84, 231–259. https://doi.org/10.1037/0033-295X.84.3.231

10. **Negativity Bias.** The tendency to give more weight to negative information than positive information.

   Example: An investor who focuses on a company's risks, rather than its potential for growth

11. **Self-Serving Bias.** The inclination to attribute positive events to one's abilities and negative events to external factors.

   Example: A salesperson who takes credit for a successful sale but blames a lost sale on the client's lack of interest.

12. **Fundamental Attribution Error.** The fundamental attribution error is a cognitive bias people use when they overemphasize dispositional (internal) explanations for other people's behavior and underestimate the role of situational (external) factors. In other words, people tend to attribute the behavior of others to their personality traits or character rather than to external circumstances that may have caused their behavior.

   Example: Suppose you see someone driving aggressively on the highway, weaving in and out of lanes and tailgating other drivers. If you make the fundamental attribution error, you might assume that the driver is rude, aggressive, and enjoys endangering others. However, there could be various situational factors influencing their behavior, such as an emergency that they're rushing to or a stressful event that just happened in their life. By assuming that their behavior is due to their personality traits, you're overlooking the possibility that external circumstances are playing a role in how they drive.

13. **Status Quo Bias.** The inclination to prefer things to remain the same rather than considering change.

Example: A company that resists updating its technology, even though it is becoming obsolete.

14. **Illusory Superiority Bias.** The disposition to overestimate one's own abilities relative to others.

Example: An investor who believes they are more knowledgeable about the stock market than the average person.

15. **Loss Aversion Bias.** The tendency to experience more pain from losses than pleasure from gains, which leads to a preference for avoiding losses rather than pursuing gains.

Example: An investor who is more likely to hold onto a losing stock in the hopes of recouping their losses than sell it and pursue other investment opportunities.

Fast Fact: A study published in the journal Healthcare (Basel) *found that loss aversion can lead individuals to delay or avoid preventative care, even when the potential benefits outweigh the costs.*[6]

16. **Herding Bias.** The tendency to follow the crowd or to mimic the actions of others rather than making independent decisions based on one's own research and analysis.

Example: An investor who invests in a particular stock simply because it's popular among other investors rather

[6] Bessey D. (2021). Loss Aversion and Health Behaviors: Results from Two Incentivized Economic Experiments. *Healthcare (Basel)*, *9*(8), 1040.

than conducting their own analysis of the company's financials and prospects. I've seen many experienced investors make the mistake of assuming their peers had conducted due diligence before investing in a particular opportunity. Big mistake!

17. **Endowment Bias.** The proneness to overvalue something simply because one owns it or has a personal attachment to it.

Example. An investor who is unwilling to sell a particular stock they own, despite evidence that it may no longer be a wise investment, simply because they have an emotional attachment to it.

Strategies for Overcoming Cognitive Biases in Decision-Making

Here are several strategies that can support you in overcoming cognitive biases in decision-making:

1. Decision Awareness

First, be aware that you are making a decision. We often don't even realize we're making decisions, let alone decisions that can be significantly and unknowingly influenced by our cognitive biases. Therefore, it is crucial that we "practice" becoming aware or mindful of decision points that arise. At the moment we become aware that a decision is needed, it is then imperative we pause and contemplate the impact that the bias may have on this decision.

2. Cognitive Bias Knowledge

There are literally hundreds of known cognitive biases. Be very curious about them, at least the most prevalent ones. The more you know about them, the more likely you are to spot them either in your own behavior and the behavior of others.

3.   Contradictory Evidence

Once aware of the bias, the next best step is to actively seek out diverse perspectives and opinions on the decision at hand, especially those that contradict your own. This process can help broaden your understanding of the issue and provide alternative viewpoints that challenge your assumptions. There are several ways this can be accomplished.

4.   Coaching

As a coach who owns and leads a coaching business, coaching is of course my favorite method of improving decision-making skills. (And yes, I am biased! That doesn't mean it's wrong, though.)

Coaches can be valuable partners in the decision-making process, providing clients with a supportive and challenging environment in which to examine their assumptions and their biases. The process of examining assumptions and biases will free the individual to consider alternative perspectives. Outstanding coaches will challenge their clients' perspectives by asking them thought-provoking questions. This process can help individuals gain a deeper understanding of themselves, their goals, and the options available to them, thus helping them make more informed decisions.

5.   Ask Open-ended Questions

Instead of asking leading questions that confirm your preconceived notions, try asking open-ended questions that allow for a variety of answers and perspectives. This interrogation can help you uncover information you may not have considered otherwise.

Here's an example of how an open-ended question could be used to challenge biases in a decision-making process:

Let's say a team is trying to decide whether to invest in a new product idea. One team member is particularly enthusiastic about the idea, while another team member is skeptical. The enthusiastic team member may have a confirmation bias, while the skeptical team member may have a negativity bias. To challenge both biases, the coach could ask an open-ended question, such as:

"What are some of the potential pros and cons of investing in this new product idea?"

This question allows both team members to share their perspectives on the idea without leading them toward a particular answer. Instead, it encourages them to think critically about the potential risks and rewards of the investment and to consider various factors that may influence the decision-making process. By exploring multiple perspectives, the team may be able to make a more informed and unbiased decision.

6. Test Assumptions

Instead of assuming that your beliefs are correct, try testing them by seeking evidence that contradicts them. This practice can help to challenge your assumptions and create a more accurate picture of the situation.

For example, a coach, an advisor, or a member of the decision-making team can challenge the assumptions from the previous example (whether to invest in a new product idea) by suggesting team members look for evidence that contradicts it. For example, they can ask questions:

- *What are the key differences between this new product and the ones we've had success with in the past?*
- *Are there any changes in the market or customer needs that could affect the success of this product?*
- *Have we conducted any market research or customer feedback on this new product?*

By asking these open-ended questions and seeking out evidence that may contradict the initial assumption, the decision-makers can test their assumptions and ensure that they are making a well-informed decision. This exercise can also help teams identify any potential biases that may be influencing the decision-making process.

7.   Consider Alternative Explanations

When considering a decision, it's important to consider alternative explanations for the situation or problem at hand. This practice can help decision-makers prevent confirmation bias by opening them up to new possibilities and perspectives.

Let's say you're trying to decide whether to invest in a particular stock. You've done your research and you believe that the stock is undervalued and poised to increase in value. However, to prevent confirmation bias, you should consider alternative explanations for why the stock might be undervalued.

For example, you could consider the possibility that the market as a whole is in a downturn and that the stock is not undervalued but rather appropriately valued given the current economic climate. You could also consider the possibility that there are factors affecting the stock that you may not be aware of, such as a pending lawsuit or regulatory investigation. By considering these alternative explanations, you can challenge your assumptions and ensure you're making a more informed decision.

8.   Seek Feedback

Getting feedback from others can help you identify blind spots and biases that may be impacting your decision-making process. This feedback can be particularly helpful when making important decisions with significant consequences.

Early on at Arootah, we needed to decide whether to implement a new software system for our project management. I was concerned that I had biases that would support keeping the system I had used for many years since I built it myself! I assumed that the new system would not be as efficient or effective. However, by seeking feedback from my team members, I learned that the current system had been causing frustration and delays. Its main flaw was that it didn't allow users to collaborate as easily as other newer systems. By considering their feedback and alternative perspectives, I realized that the new system could improve productivity and morale. This feedback led me to make a better decision overall, and, with hindsight, I'm confident it was the right decision. Further, this also led us to improve our project management software through which we expanded on the collaboration features.

9. Healthy Debate

Another key strategy for overcoming the challenges of cognitive bias in decision-making is to encourage *healthy* debate. A healthy debate involves presenting different perspectives and challenging each other's assumptions and beliefs while maintaining a respectful and open-minded approach.

In the context of financial analysis and decision-making, this is commonly referred to as presenting "The Bull and Bear Case." It requires considering both positive and negative outlooks and can help to prevent confirmation bias by forcing one to consider multiple perspectives and potential outcomes.

When having these debates, it is important to set up the "rules of engagement." These rules help to ensure that the debate is productive and respectful and does not devolve into personal attacks or heated arguments. It's also important to remember that the goal of a healthy debate is not to "win" or prove one's own point but rather to arrive at the best possible decision or solution. After the debate is over, it's important to come together and move forward as a team, regardless of who "won" the debate.

This approach is akin to the leadership principle of "disagree and commit," popularized by Jeff Bezos, the founder of Amazon. The principle is based on the idea that when a decision needs to be made, it's important to have healthy debate and discussion to ensure that all perspectives and ideas are considered. Once a decision is made, however, even if someone disagrees with it, they should commit to it and support it wholeheartedly.

> *At my hedge fund Blue Ridge Capital, my partner, John, would often use the principle of "strong opinions, weakly held" to help negate the impact that cognitive bias had on deciding which stocks to pick. I quickly adopted it as my own as well once I saw the potential impact of teaching this mindset. He had learned this strategy from his Stanford professor. It essentially suggests that one should have a clear and strong initial opinion on a particular topic*

or issue. Still, it should be open to immediately changing that opinion if presented with more convincing information or evidence. This approach means being confident and assertive in your beliefs while also being willing to admit when you are wrong or change your position when new or better information is presented. The phrase "strong opinions, weakly held" is often used in the context of decision-making and problem-solving, as it encourages individuals to have conviction and take action (as you will learn about later) while also being open to feedback and adjusting course if necessary.

Overall, healthy debate can be a powerful tool for overcoming cognitive bias by challenging assumptions and beliefs and allowing for the consideration of multiple perspectives and potential outcomes.

Conclusion

Cognitive biases are inherent flaws in the way humans process information and make judgments, and they can lead to errors in decision-making. They are a product of how our brains have evolved to process information and make decisions in the face of incomplete or ambiguous data. While they can lead to errors and mistakes in judgment, they are also a necessary component of our ability to navigate the complex and the often uncertain world around us.

To overcome the obstacle of cognitive biases in decision-making, it is essential to be aware of decision points and acquire knowledge about the most prevalent cognitive biases. Seeking out diverse perspectives and opinions, testing assumptions, considering alternative explanations, and getting feedback from others can also help you identify blind spots and biases. Healthy debate, presented as "The Bull and Bear Case," can be a powerful tool for challenging assumptions and beliefs and considering multiple perspectives and potential outcomes.

The leadership principle of "disagree and commit" and the strategy of "strong opinions, weakly held" can help to negate the impact that cognitive biases have on making decisions. By being

confident and assertive in your beliefs, while also being open to feedback and adjusting course, if necessary, you can have conviction and take action toward the best possible decision or solution.

Summary

1. Cognitive biases are unconscious patterns of thought that can lead to errors in judgment and decision-making.
2. There are many different types of cognitive biases, including confirmation bias, availability bias, and anchoring bias.
3. These biases can impact our decisions in various ways, from leading us to ignore important information to causing us to overestimate our abilities.
4. One common way cognitive biases can impact our decisions is by leading us to make choices consistent with our pre-existing beliefs or opinions.
5. To overcome cognitive biases in decision making, it's essential to be aware of them and actively seek out diverse perspectives and contradictory evidence.
6. Seeking feedback from others and testing assumptions can also help us identify blind spots and biases.
7. Coaching can be a valuable tool in helping individuals examine their assumptions and biases and make more informed decisions.
8. Asking open-ended questions and considering alternative explanations can help us prevent confirmation bias and encourage critical thinking.
9. Cognitive biases are a natural part of human cognition, but we can make better decisions by being mindful of them and taking steps to overcome them.
10. It's important to note that overcoming cognitive biases is an ongoing process requiring continuous effort and self-reflection.

Questions

1. What are cognitive biases?

    Errors in thinking that can lead to inaccurate decision-making.

2. How can cognitive biases impact our decisions?

    By distorting our perceptions, beliefs, and attitudes.

3. What are some common types of cognitive biases?

    Confirmation, availability, anchoring, and framing bias.

4. What is confirmation bias?

    The tendency to seek out and interpret information in a way that confirms one's pre-existing beliefs.

5. How can seeking out diverse perspectives help us overcome cognitive biases?

    By exposing us to alternative viewpoints.

6. What is coaching, and how can it help individuals make better decisions?

    Coaching is a process of providing guidance, support, and feedback to help individuals improve their performance.

7. What are some strategies for testing assumptions and challenging biases?

    Seeking out contrary evidence, considering more explanations.

8. How can open-ended questions stimulate critical thinking?

    By promoting reflection, exploration, and creativity, and helping individuals avoid simplistic or binary answers.

9. Why is it important to consider alternative explanations when making decisions?

    It helps us to mitigate the effects of cognitive biases.

10. Why is it important to be mindful of biases?

    It helps us to avoid errors and improve accuracy and effectiveness.

Exercises

1. Identify examples of confirmation bias in everyday situations and explore how they could have been avoided.

2. Analyze a recent decision you made and identify any potential cognitive biases that may have influenced your thinking.

3. Practice seeking out and considering alternative perspectives on a current issue or problem.

4. Use open-ended questions to prompt critical thinking and explore different angles of a decision.

5. Read about and research different types of cognitive biases and their impact on decision-making.

6. Play devil's advocate and actively challenge your own assumptions and beliefs.

7. Ask for feedback from others and consider their perspectives when making decisions.

8. Test assumptions by seeking out data and evidence that contradicts your initial beliefs.

9. Develop a decision-making process that includes steps for identifying and addressing cognitive biases.

10. Reflect on past decisions and consider how awareness of cognitive biases could have improved outcomes.

Principle 3

Balance System 1 and System 2 Thinking

*"System 1 operates automatically and quickly,
with little or no effort and no sense of voluntary
control. System 2 allocates attention to the effortful
mental activities that demand it, including
complex computations. The operations of System 2
are often associated with the subjective experience
of agency, choice, and concentration."*

*— Daniel Kahneman (on the differences between
the types of thinking we use to make decisions)*

Finding the Right Mix for Optimal Outcomes

We have two systems of thinking. System 1 entails fast, intuitive, and automatic thinking, while System 2 is a slower, deliberate, and more analytical thought process. It's important to balance both thinking systems because relying solely on one can result in biased or incomplete decisions. By using both thinking systems, we can better understand our biases, weigh available information, and make more well-rounded, effective decisions.

Key Question
*How can we effectively balance the strengths and
weaknesses of System 1 and System 2 thinking to
avoid biases and errors when making decisions?*

Effective decision-making is a crucial skill in both our personal and professional lives as well as in the businesses we operate. However, not all decisions are created equal. Some require quick, intuitive thinking and are made on the fly, while others benefit from a more methodical and deliberate approach. Given

that the average person has an estimated 6,000 thoughts per day, it's no surprise many decisions are made in a matter of seconds or less.[7]

In this chapter, we'll explore the two primary categories of *conscious* decision-making processes:

1. Those that are made "in the moment."
2. Those that allow for more time and deliberation

We'll also examine the strengths and weaknesses of each approach and discuss how to strike a balance between them for optimal decision-making.

In the first chapter of the international bestseller *Thinking, Fast and Slow*,[8] Daniel Kahneman introduced the concept of two systems of thinking:

- **System 1**, which is fast and intuitive
- **System 2**, which is slow and deliberate

He argues that System 1 thinking is often the default mode of human cognition and is necessary for survival and everyday decision-making. However, System 1 thinking can also lead to cognitive biases and errors in judgment, particularly in situations that require System 2 thinking. Kahneman suggests that individuals can improve their decision-making skills and avoid common pitfalls by becoming aware of these biases and learning to engage in more deliberate, System 2 thinking. The conclusion of Chapter 1 emphasizes the importance of understanding the strengths and weaknesses of each system of thinking and

---

[7] Halvorson, H. G. (2022, December 16). How to Recognize Negative Thought Loops and Stop Obsessing. Psychology Today. https://www.psychologytoday.com/us/blog/the-stories-we-tell/202212/how-to-recognize-negative-thought-loops-and-stop-obsessing

[8] Kahneman, D. (2011). *Thinking, Fast and Slow*. Farrar, Straus and Giroux.

learning to use them in balance to make more informed decisions.

System 1 thinking is largely automatic and unconscious and occurs in areas of the brain that are evolutionarily older and more primitive, such as the amygdala and basal ganglia.

On the other hand, **System 2** thinking requires conscious effort and is associated with the more recently evolved prefrontal cortex, which is responsible for higher-order cognitive processes. So, in essence, System 1 thinking can be thought of as more closely related to automatic, preconscious processes, while System 2 thinking is associated with more deliberative, conscious processes.[9]

Fast thinking (System 1) is often most suitable for situations where quick decisions are needed, such as:

- Emergency situations where a rapid response is required to avoid danger or prevent harm.
- Day-to-day activities that require quick and automatic decision-making, such as driving a car or walking down the street.
- Situations in which there is little time for reflection or analysis, such as in competitive sports or negotiations.

Slow thinking (System 2), on the other hand, is most suitable for situations where careful consideration is required, such as:

---

[9] While the terms "System 1" and "System 2" in Kahneman's model primarily refer to two modes of thinking related to *cognitive processes*, it is also important to note that there are many bodily processes that occur *unconsciously*, such as the beating of our hearts and the regulation of blood flow. These bodily processes are typically controlled by the autonomic nervous system, which is responsible for regulating many involuntary bodily functions. It is important to note that these types of decisions are different from the types of decisions that are made through *cognitive processes*, as they are not typically subject to conscious thought or decision-making.

- Complex problems that require analysis and evaluation of multiple factors, such as financial planning or business strategy.
- Situations that involve significant risk or uncertainty, such as major investments or medical treatments.
- Ethical or moral dilemmas that require reflection and careful consideration of values and principles.

In general, fast thinking is more suitable for routine or familiar situations, while slow thinking is most suitable for novel or complex situations that require careful consideration and analysis. However, it is important to note that both types of thinking are necessary for effective decision-making and should be used in balance.

When faced with a decision, our first instinct or impulse is often to rely on System 1 thinking (reflexive). This kind of thinking can help us efficiently navigate many aspects of daily life. It allows us to quickly and automatically process large amounts of information and make decisions without engaging in deliberate, conscious thought. However, relying too heavily on System 1 thinking can lead to errors and biases, leaving us prone to making snap judgments and ignoring important information that may be relevant to a decision. Therefore, it is important to balance System 1 and System 2 thinking to make well-informed and accurate decisions.

Pause and Reflect

When faced with a decision that requires more deliberate and analytical thinking, it can be helpful to **"pause and reflect"** in order to engage in System 2 thinking. This process involves taking a step back from the immediate situation, gathering additional information or evidence, and deliberately considering different options and potential outcomes before making a decision. This kind of reflection is particularly important when making complex or high-stakes decisions, as it can help to mitigate the effects of biases and heuristics (or cognitive shortcuts) associated with System 1 thinking.

The concept of "pause and reflect" in decision making is similar to the concept Viktor Frankl discusses in his book *Man's Search for Meaning*. In his approach to psychotherapy, which he called "logotherapy," Frankl emphasizes the importance of finding meaning and purpose in life, particularly in the face of difficult or challenging circumstances.[10] Part of this process involves taking a step back from your immediate situation and reflecting on your values and goals in order to make deliberate and intentional decisions that are aligned with your sense of purpose and meaning. While Frankl's approach is focused on a broader sense of life purpose, the concept of "pause and reflect" can also be applied in the context of more specific decision-making situations in order to engage System 2 thinking and make well-informed choices.

Let's take a look at a real-life example of this process.

An employee approaches their boss with a new idea for a project, but the boss is feeling stressed and overwhelmed by other tasks and immediately feels annoyed at being approached with yet another demand on his time. The boss's initial impulse is to dismiss the idea and tell the employee to come back later. However, he recognizes this as a moment where his emotions might be getting in the way of good decision-making, so he takes a deep breath and consciously shifts into System 2 thinking.

In this moment of reflection, the boss reminds himself that it is important to listen to new ideas from the team, even if he's busy, and that dismissing the employee's idea out of hand could damage the employee's motivation and engagement in their work. The boss takes a few minutes to ask the employee some questions about their idea to better understand its potential value and feasibility. The boss then tells the employee that he will need time to think about the idea and consider how it might fit into the company's overall priorities and workload.

---

[10] Frankl, V. E. (2006). Man's Search for Meaning: An Introduction to Logotherapy. Beacon Press.

By pausing and reflecting, the boss is able to move beyond his initial emotional reaction and engage in more thoughtful and deliberate decision making. This helps him to make a better-informed choice about whether or not to pursue the employee's idea while maintaining a positive and productive relationship with their team members.

Of course, it's not always easy to catch yourself before the emotion and System 1 thinking takes over, and it does take practice to develop the skill of mindfulness and the ability to shift into System 2 thinking.

Mindfulness

Mindfulness is the practice of paying attention to the present moment with openness, curiosity, and non-judgment. It involves being aware of your thoughts, feelings, and bodily sensations without overly identifying with them. Mindfulness can help individuals catch themselves when they are experiencing strong emotions, or are being triggered by certain situations, so they can become more intentional in their responses. Meditation is often mentioned in the same vein as mindfulness. A review published in the journal *Psychological Medicine* found that mindfulness meditation was associated with improved emotional regulation and decision-making abilities.[11]

In the context of decision-making, mindfulness can be a useful tool for recognizing when your emotions are influencing your thought processes and for intentionally shifting into System 2 thinking to make a more rational and deliberate choice. By practicing mindfulness regularly, individuals can become more adept at recognizing their emotional reactions and consciously choosing how to respond to each situation. Studies have shown that regular meditation practice can increase activity in the prefrontal cortex, a brain region associated with cognitive

---

[11] Shapiro, S., Jazaieri, H., & Goldin, P. (2012) Mindfulness-based stress reduction effects on moral reasoning and decision making. The Journal of Positive Psychology 7(6), 504-515

control, attention, and decision-making. This increased activity
has been linked to better decision-making abilities.[12]

Malcolm Gladwell propounds in his book *Blink* that our ability
to make quick, intuitive decisions, what he calls "thin-slicing"
(System 1), can be just as powerful as our more deliberate,
analytical (System 2) thinking.[13] He believes that our
subconscious mind can process vast amounts of information
and quickly arrive at accurate conclusions, even when we don't
consciously understand how we arrived at those conclusions.

Gladwell presents numerous examples of situations in which
people were able to make quick, accurate judgments based on
minimal information, such as art experts identifying a fake
painting at a glance or professional tennis players making split-
second decisions about where to hit the ball. He argues that, in
these situations, our subconscious mind is drawing on a wealth
of experience and expertise and can quickly identify patterns and
make connections that our conscious mind may not be able to
discern.

However, Gladwell also acknowledges that this type of thinking
can be influenced by unconscious biases and can lead to errors
in judgment, particularly in situations where we may not have
enough information or where our emotions are highly engaged.
He writes that it's important to be aware of these potential
pitfalls and to consciously evaluate our thinking processes to
ensure we make the best decisions possible.

Here are some examples of situations where thin-slicing (or
"rapid, intuitive decision-making") can be effective:

- Experienced hedge fund managers could make a
  "blink" decision when they quickly decide to invest in a
  particular stock.

---

12 Ibid.
13 Gladwell, M. (2007). *Blink: The Power of Thinking Without Thinking*.
Back Bay Books.

- Experienced firefighters often rapidly assess a situation and determine whether a building is safe to enter or whether a particular course of action is likely to be effective.
- Professional athletes can make split-second decisions during a game.
- Experienced doctors and nurses can diagnose a patient's condition based on a few key symptoms, allowing them to provide timely and effective treatment.
- A skilled chef may be able to taste a dish and adjust the seasoning or other ingredients.

The individuals in each of these situations have developed a high level of expertise and experience in their respective fields, allowing them to make quick and accurate judgments based on limited information. However, it's important to note that this type of decision-making can *still* be influenced by biases and other factors, and it may still be prudent to make such decisions in conjunction with more deliberate, analytical thinking when appropriate.

Overall, Gladwell's view is that our ability to make quick, intuitive judgments can be a powerful tool in decision-making for those who have experience in the relevant subject matter, but it must be balanced with a conscious awareness of our thought processes and a willingness to acknowledge and address potential biases.

I was fortunate to meet with Gladwell a short time ago. When questioned about whether his work differed from Kahneman's in the sense that System 2 thinking should be used for what one would assume would be a more deliberative type of a decision, he said that "no," they were aligned. He added that this type of quick, intuitive thinking ("thin-slicing") is most effective when individuals have a *high level of expertise and experience in a particular area*. He argues that our subconscious mind can draw on this experience to quickly identify patterns and make accurate judgments based on limited information.

However, like Kahneman, he also cautions that this type of thinking can be influenced by unconscious biases and can lead to errors in judgment, particularly in situations where we may not have enough information or where our emotions are highly engaged. Therefore, it's important to be aware of these potential pitfalls and consciously evaluate our thinking processes to ensure we make the best decisions possible. He said that many, if not most, readers misinterpreted his work to mean that *every decision* could be made with their "blink." He said it was almost like they had read a different book entirely! They somehow missed the part where he notes that this type of thinking is best used by *experts who have developed a high level of expertise and experience in their respective fields.* It is not to be used by everybody.

I was also fortunate enough to meet with Annie Duke (*How to Decide* and *Thinking in Bets*) and Daniel Kahneman at a charity event.[14] Kahneman said that Gladwell's views were largely compatible with respect to the benefits and limitations of fast and slow thinking; it's just that Gladwell focused more on the benefits of fast thinking.

Balance System 1 and System 2 Thinking

A simple process to "Pause and Reflect" for effectively balancing the strengths and weaknesses of System 1 and System 2 thinking when making decisions could be as follows:

1. Knowledge of biases: Make the investment in time to educate yourself on Cognitive Biases that can impact your decision-making so that you can spot them.
2. Recognize the situation: Become aware of the decision-making situation and identify whether it requires quick,

---

[14] Alliance for Decision Education. A wonderful organization co-founded by Annie that empowers students with essential skills and dispositions for making better decisions.

intuitive thinking (System 1) or more deliberate, analytical thinking (System 2).

3. Pause: Take a moment to pause and consciously shift your focus from the automatic response (System 1) to a more reflective state (System 2).

4. Gather information: Collect relevant information and data to help inform your decision-making process. Be aware of any potential biases that could influence your interpretation of the information.

5. Identify biases and heuristics: Recognize any cognitive biases or mental shortcuts that may be at play in the current situation, and consider how they might be affecting your judgment.

6. Reflect: Take the time to think through the decision carefully, weighing the pros and cons of each option and considering possible consequences. Then, reflect on your thought process and ensure you're not being swayed by biases or relying solely on intuition.

7. Evaluate alternatives: Assess different options and potential solutions, taking into account both the information you've gathered and the insights from your reflection.

8. Make a decision: After careful consideration, make a well-informed decision based on the balanced use of System 1 and System 2 thinking.

9. Monitor the outcome: Once you've made your decision, pay attention to the results and assess whether the decision was effective.

10. Adjust your mental model: If necessary, adjust your approach and learn from the experience to improve your decision-making in the future.

By following this Pause and Reflect process, you can consciously shift between System 1 and System 2, thinking as needed, helping you avoid biases and errors and make better-informed decisions.

Conclusion

Understanding the differences between System 1 and System 2 thinking and learning to use them in balance is crucial for effective decision-making. Fast thinking (System 1) can be effective in routine or familiar situations that require quick and automatic decisions, while slow thinking (System 2), is most suitable for complex or high-stakes decisions that require careful consideration and analysis. However, it is important to note that both types of thinking are necessary depending on context.

Being mindful of your thought processes and emotions and intentionally shifting into System 2 thinking when necessary can help you avoid common biases and errors in judgment.

Furthermore, while "thin-slicing" (rapid, intuitive decision-making) can be effective in certain situations for experts who have developed a high level of expertise, it is important to acknowledge and address potential biases and to consciously evaluate your thinking processes to ensure that you are making the best decisions possible.

Summary

1. Decision-making is an important skill that requires a balance between quick and deliberate thinking.
2. System 1 thinking is fast and intuitive, while System 2 thinking is slow and deliberate.
3. System 1 thinking is associated with the subconscious processes of the brain, while System 2 thinking is associated with the conscious processes of the brain.
4. Fast thinking is most suitable for routine situations, while slow thinking is more suitable for complex situations.
5. Relying too heavily on System 1 thinking can lead to errors and biases.
6. To engage System 2 thinking, it can be helpful to "pause and reflect" before making a decision.
7. "Pause and reflect" is similar to the concept of logotherapy, which emphasizes finding meaning and purpose in life.
8. Both System 1 and System 2 thinking is necessary for effective decision-making.
9. Fast thinking is suitable for emergency situations and day-to-day activities, while slow thinking is suitable for complex problems and ethical dilemmas.
10. Using both types of thinking in balance can lead one to make more informed and accurate decisions.

Questions

1. What are the two primary categories of decision-making?

   Intuitive thinking (System 1) or deliberate thinking (System 2).

2. What are the strengths and weaknesses of each approach?

   System 1 is fast and efficient, but prone to biases. System 2 is more deliberate, but can be slow and resource intensive.

3. What is System 1 thinking?

   It is intuitive, automatic, and often subconscious.

4. What is System 2 thinking?

   It is analytical, deliberate, and conscious.

5. When is fast thinking most suitable in decision-making?

   When the situation is familiar, and there is limited time or information available.

6. When is slow thinking most suitable for decision-making?

   When the situation is complex, and there is time to analyze information.

7. What are the potential drawbacks of relying too heavily on System 1 thinking?

   It can lead to biases, errors, and irrational decision-making.

8. What is the concept of "pause and reflect" in decision-making?

   Taking a moment to step back, consider alternative perspectives, and evaluate potential consequences.

9. How is "pause and reflect" similar to logotherapy?

   They both involve reflecting on one's values, goals, and a sense of purpose.

10. Why is it important to use both System 1 and System 2?

   It allows for a more accurate decision-making process.

Exercises

1. Consider a decision you made recently and determine whether you used System 1 or System 2 thinking.
2. Reflect on situations where you rely more on System 1 thinking and situations where you rely more on System 2 thinking.
3. Practice "pausing and reflecting" before making a decision today and identify any new information or options considered as a result.
4. Identify potential biases or errors that could result from relying heavily on System 1 thinking in a decision-making situation.
5. Recall a previous decision impacted by a cognitive bias and consider how System 2 thinking could have been used to mitigate its effects.
6. Evaluate the decision-making process for a recent major purchase and assess whether you relied more on System 1 or System 2 thinking and explain why.
7. Consider how logotherapy could be useful in making difficult decisions.
8. Determine how to balance System 1 and System 2 thinking when making a decision that involves both routine and complex aspects.
9. Identify potential benefits of relying more on System 2 thinking in daily decision-making.
10. Apply the concept of "pause and reflect" in a group decision-making setting.

Principle 4

Pause and Reflect on Emotions

"Don't let your emotions overpower your intelligence."

- T.I., Slide Show

Conscious Intervention and Emotional Regulation

The Pause and Reflect Strategy involves taking a moment to step back when a trigger presents itself to make a decision and then reflect before making that decision, especially in high-stress situations where emotions are heightened. This strategy helps you break the cycle of emotional decision-making, regain control of your emotions, and make more rational, logical choices. By utilizing this principle, you can improve your decision-making abilities and help you avoid making impulsive or regretful decisions.

Key Question
How can we develop greater awareness and control over our emotional responses to make more intentional, logical, and constructive choices in our personal and professional lives?

Emotions

Emotions have a powerful impact on the decisions we make, often leading us to make choices that are not in our best interests. A survey conducted by the American Psychological Association found that 38% of adults make decisions based on emotions rather than facts or logic.[15] When we make decisions based on emotions rather than rational thinking, we run the risk of making poor choices that can have negative consequences on our lives and the lives of others.

Why? Because emotions can cloud our judgment and cause us to focus on short-term gains or immediate gratification rather than considering the long-term consequences of our decisions. We may make impulsive purchases we can't afford. We may react to a situation without considering the consequences of our reactions.

It's important to note that not all emotions have a negative impact on decision-making. Positive emotions, such as happiness and excitement, can lead to more creative thinking and better problem-solving. However, while positive emotions can be beneficial, they can also lead us astray by causing us to be overconfident or biased towards optimism, causing us to ignore negative feedback, or causing us to act impulsively. It's often negative emotions, such as fear, anger, and anxiety, that people associate with leading them astray. However, even though negative emotions can be uncomfortable, they can also serve essential functions and be beneficial in certain situations.

For example, fear or anxiety can motivate us to take action and address a problem or challenge, while anger or frustration can alert us to an unfair situation that needs to be addressed. Experiencing guilt or regret can lead us to evaluate our choices and make changes to future behavior. Sadness or grief can help us connect with others who have experienced loss by offering support and comfort. By learning to accept and manage our negative emotions, we can develop resilience, empathy, and a greater capacity for growth and learning. So, despite each emotion's reputation, in reality, *both* positive and negative

---

[15] American Psychological Association. (2015). *Stress in America: Paying with our health.*
http://www.apa.org/news/press/releases/stress/2014/stress-report.pdf.

emotions can either lead us in the right direction or way off course.

Furthermore, our emotional responses can be influenced by modern factors that aren't relevant to the decision at hand, such as past experiences, biases, and societal or cultural norms. These factors can lead us to make decisions that aren't based on accurate information or rational thought, but instead on an emotional response that may not be appropriate for the situation.

For example, a person who has a fear of flying may decide to avoid traveling by air, even if it means missing out on important opportunities or experiences. While their emotional *response* is understandable given their fear, it is almost certainly not the best *decision* for their overall well-being and goals since it is fairly well-known flying is one of the safest forms of transportation.

We are more likely to make emotional decisions over logical ones when our emotions are heightened. For example, according to a study published in the *Annual Review of Psychology*, people are more likely to make emotional decisions when they are tired or stressed.[16] Similarly, according to a study by the University of Chicago's Booth School of Business, people are more likely to make emotional decisions when they are in a positive mood, such as after receiving good news.[17] (My team somehow figured this one out. I eventually caught on to the idea that my team would wait for some amazing news at our firm when they wanted to ask me for something big, knowing I would give in more quickly if I was in a great mood!)

Fortunately, by understanding the ways in which emotions can impact our decision making, we can learn to recognize when our

---

[16] Lerner, J. S., Li, Y., Valdesolo, P., & Kassam, K. S. (2015). Emotion and decision making. *Annual Review of Psychology*, 66, 799-823.

[17] Isen, A. M., & Patrick, R. (1983). The effect of positive feelings on risk-taking: When the chips are down. *Organizational Behavior and Human Performance*, 31 (2), 194-202.

emotions are influencing our choices and take steps to ensure that our decisions are based on rational thinking and sound judgment. Emotions can be a valuable tool in decision making, but they can also be a hindrance if we rely solely on them to help us make choices. Understanding the role of emotions in decision making and developing strategies to mitigate their negative impact is crucial for making quality decisions that align with our goals and values.

What Are the Signals of our Emotions?

Let's explore the ten most common positive and negative emotions, the signals they provide us that can either guide us in the right direction or lead us astray, and examples of how they can impact our decision making. From the destructive force of anger to the paralyzing effect of love, understanding these emotions and their impact on decision making is key to making better choices.

Positive Emotions

- **Happiness.** Signals that things are going well and promote a desire to maintain the status quo or seek out similar positive experiences. However, happiness can lead to complacency and a failure to take risks that may ultimately lead to growth and improvement. For example, sticking to a comfortable routine and avoiding new opportunities.
- **Love.** Indicates connection and attachment to others and promotes behaviors that reinforce those connections. However, love can lead us to a lack of objectivity and poor decision-making regarding those we love. For example, staying in a toxic relationship due to feelings of love and attachment.
- **Gratitude.** Shows appreciation for what we have and promotes behaviors that reinforce those sources of gratitude. However, this can also lead you to a reluctance to make changes or take risks that may lead to greater opportunities for growth and fulfillment. For

example, someone may choose to stay in an unfulfilling job due to financial stability, feeling grateful simply for having a job in the first place.

- **Contentment.** Marks satisfaction with a current situation and promotes behaviors that maintain that status quo. However, this can also lead to a lack of ambition and a failure to pursue goals and aspirations that may lead to greater fulfillment and satisfaction. For example, a person might settle for a mediocre job or lifestyle due to contentment with their current situation.

- **Excitement.** Signals anticipation and eagerness for new experiences and promotes behaviors through which you can seek out those experiences. However, this can also lead to impulsive decision-making and a failure to consider the potential risks and consequences of those experiences. For example, someone might make impulsive purchases or take on excessive risks without considering the potential consequences.

- **Pride.** Denotes a sense of accomplishment and promotes behaviors that reinforce that sense of accomplishment. However, pride can also lead to arrogance and a failure to acknowledge and learn from mistakes or setbacks. For example, an individual might refuse to seek feedback or help from others due to a sense of pride in one's abilities.

- **Curiosity.** Manifests as a desire for new knowledge and experiences and promotes behaviors that allow us to seek out those opportunities. However, curiosity can also lead to distraction and a failure to focus on important tasks or responsibilities. For example, spending excessive time exploring new hobbies or interests rather than focusing on work or school responsibilities.

- **Hope.** Signals a belief in the possibility of positive outcomes and promotes behaviors that push us toward those outcomes. However, hope can also lead to unrealistic expectations and a failure to recognize and prepare for potential obstacles and setbacks. For example, we may expect immediate success or instant gratification rather than recognizing the time and effort required to achieve long-term goals.

- **Confidence.** Indicates a belief in a person's abilities and promotes behaviors that reinforce that belief. However, this can also lead to overconfidence and a failure to acknowledge and address weaknesses or limitations. For example, taking on tasks or responsibilities beyond our abilities due to overconfidence.

- **Inspiration.** Signals a sense of motivation and drive to pursue goals and aspirations and promotes behaviors that support that pursuit. However, inspiration can also lead to a reliance on external sources of motivation and a failure to develop intrinsic motivation and self-discipline. For example, relying solely on external motivational factors such as rewards or recognition rather than developing intrinsic motivation and discipline.

Negative Emotions

- **Fear.** Indicates a potential threat (danger) and leads individuals to PREPARE (i.e., fight or flee). However, fear can also lead us to irrational and exaggerated fears that limit our personal growth and opportunities. For example, you might avoid flying on airplanes due to fear of flying, even though statistically, it is a safe mode of transportation.

- **Anger.** Denotes that our principles have been violated in some way and drives us to fight to remedy this. However, anger can also lead to aggressive or violent behavior that can be harmful to oneself or others. For example, physically lashing out at someone who has made a minor mistake.

- **Sadness.** Marks a sense of loss or unfulfilled expectations and drives us to withdraw. However, sadness can also lead to prolonged periods of isolation and inactivity that can exacerbate negative emotions. For example, we might withdraw from social activities for an extended period after a loss.

- **Guilt.** Results from a personal violation of our moral code and drives us to make amends. However, guilt can also lead some individuals to overcompensate and put the needs of others above their own. For example, you might constantly say yes to others' requests or demands out of guilt, even if the requests go against your own values or goals.

- **Shame.** Indicates a sense of inadequacy or failure and drives us to hide. However, shame can also lead us to avoid important opportunities and relationships, and self-sabotage. For example, we might avoid public speaking or other situations that could lead to success and growth due to our fear of failure.

- **Jealousy.** Signals a threat to a valued relationship or possession and drives us to protect it. However, jealousy can also lead us to possessive and controlling behaviors that can be harmful to the relationship or the individual. For example, an individual who monitors their partner's every move or limits their interactions with others out of jealousy damages their partner and the relationship.

- **Envy.** Manifests from a desire for something someone else has and drives us to acquire it. However, envy can also lead to destructive behavior, such as resentment or attempts to sabotage others' success. For example, spreading rumors about a coworker who received a promotion they desired.

- **Disgust.** Shows a revulsion towards something or someone and drives us away from the situation. However, disgust can also lead to prejudice and discrimination against individuals or groups. For example, discriminating against someone due to their race or ethnicity.

- **Frustration.** Signals an obstacle or barrier to a desired outcome and drives us to persist or give up. However, frustration can also lead a person to impulsiveness or rash decision-making that may not be in their best interest. For example, quitting a job impulsively due to frustration with a coworker or supervisor.

- **Anxiety.** Derives from an uncertain or potentially dangerous situation and drives us to prepare for or avoid it. However, anxiety can also lead us to avoid important opportunities or relationships and to self-sabotage. For example, we might avoid travel or social situations due to anxiety, even though they may benefit us in the long run.

Emotional Regulation

Emotions are a natural and integral part of human life, and they play a significant role in shaping our behavior and decisions. They serve as our internal guidance system, signaling us to respond to certain stimuli. Positive emotions, such as happiness and contentment, often indicate that we are on the right path and encourage us to continue moving in that direction, as this was critical for our survival in the past. Negative emotions, on the other hand, such as anger and fear, often indicate that we are on the wrong path and encourage us to "course correct" toward behavior and actions that will be more conducive to our survival. These signals were critical for our survival in the past and, to a lesser degree, may be important even now. However, far more diligence must be conducted in monitoring and regulating these emotions. Emotions are often programmed for immediate gratification, which may not be in our best interests in the long term or even in the short term. Our prefrontal cortex, the part of the brain responsible for making decisions, plays a crucial role in assessing whether our emotional responses align with our overall goals and interests. It enables us to override our immediate emotional reactions and make decisions that serve our best interests in the long term.

Therefore, understanding and managing our emotions is essential for making effective decisions. Regulating our emotional responses and thinking logically and rationally can help us navigate complex situations and make decisions that lead to positive outcomes. It is only by learning to balance our emotions with our intellect that we can achieve optimal decision-making and reach our full potential.

Conscious Intervention

The term "conscious intervention" refers to the intentional and deliberate effort to interrupt automatic or habitual thought patterns and behaviors to make more informed and intentional choices. It can also refer to the process of intentionally introducing new thought patterns or behaviors that are more aligned with one's goals and values.

The idea of conscious intervention has roots in various fields of psychology, including cognitive psychology and mindfulness-based therapies. In cognitive psychology, conscious intervention is often used to help individuals recognize and challenge negative thought patterns and replace them with more positive and constructive ones. In mindfulness-based therapies, conscious intervention is used to help individuals develop greater awareness and attention to their thoughts, feelings, and behaviors to make more intentional choices and reduce automatic or habitual patterns of reactivity.

In everyday life, conscious intervention can take many forms, such as taking a moment to pause and reflect before reacting to a situation, consciously choosing to engage in behaviors that promote well-being, or intentionally setting goals and priorities that are aligned with one's values. By practicing conscious intervention, individuals can become more aware of their thoughts and behaviors and develop a greater capacity for intentional decision-making and personal growth.

The Puppeteer's Mindset: Conscious Decision-Making

The concept of conscious intervention can be beautifully illustrated through the metaphor of a marionette puppet guided by an unbiased puppeteer. Imagine the puppeteer as a rational, detached decision-maker, unburdened by cognitive biases, past experiences, or emotional baggage. Just like the marionette, we, too, can learn to approach decision-making with a fresh perspective, free from the constraints of our past experiences and biases.

Take, for example, a young man who faces rejection from someone he is interested in. This rejection might cause him to hesitate or feel anxious about approaching someone new, fearing a similar outcome. However, if the young man were a marionette controlled by an unbiased puppeteer, the puppeteer would simply guide him to try his luck with the next person, unencumbered by the pain of the previous rejection.

By adopting the mindset of the puppeteer, we can strive to make more rational decisions and consciously intervene in our thought processes, mitigating the effects of cognitive biases and emotional baggage. We can learn to evaluate each situation on its own merits, allowing us to make informed decisions that are not clouded by past experiences or preconceived notions. In essence, the marionette puppet metaphor serves as a reminder of the power of conscious intervention in shaping our decision-making processes. By consciously intervening in our thoughts and actions, we can overcome the limitations imposed by cognitive biases and emotions, allowing us to make better choices that align with our goals and values. Ultimately, embracing the puppeteer's mindset empowers us to take control of our lives and achieve greater success and fulfillment.

Emotional Decision Pathway Model (the "Cause-and-Effect" Cycle)

A careful examination of the "cause and effect" cycle reveals a sequence unfolding in our minds. Initiated by a "cause," this sequence leads to an "effect" after a series of complex processes. Within this sequence, we encounter three pivotal decisions:

1. What does this mean?
2. How should I feel about it?
3. How should I react?

These decisions can be made either consciously or subconsciously. However, our subconscious often defaults to decisions governed by survival instincts, which, as previously mentioned, often do not lead to optimal outcomes that serve our best interests in our current environment. Our success in navigating various situations depends on our ability to be mindfully aware of these decision points and effectively regulate our emotions. For example, when faced with a challenging task at work, being mindful and managing our emotions can help us override our subconscious survival instincts, allowing us to make better decisions that lead to positive outcomes. In the following sections, we will explore the *six stages* of this cycle in detail, which will all occur without any conscious interventions to the process.

1. Cause (Stimulus or Trigger)
The first step in the sequence is the stimulus or trigger. This is the event or situation that causes an individual to react or make a decision. The trigger can be anything from a sudden change in circumstances, such as losing a job, to a more mundane event, such as deciding what to have for dinner.

2. Meaning Appraisal (What does this mean?)
The second step of the cycle involves attaching meaning to the trigger. In other words, the subconscious mind does an appraisal and literally decides, with lightning speed, the meaning to attach to the stimulus. Something happens, and we ask: "What does it mean?" Our decision is based upon and influenced by a combination of psychological factors:

    i.   Experiences and Memories
    ii.   Beliefs and Mindsets

Experiences and Memories

Experiences. Past experiences shape our reactions to new situations. Experiences refer to the events, situations, or interactions that an individual goes through in their life. These experiences can be positive, negative, or neutral and contribute to shaping an individual's understanding of the world, their beliefs, values, and expectations. For example, if a person has had positive outcomes when taking risks in the past, they may be more likely to *decide* to take risks in the future.

Memories. Both conscious and unconscious memories can influence our interpretation of a situation. Note that memories differ from experiences. Memories are the mental *representations* of past experiences stored in the brain. They are recollections of these events that we can access at a later time. Memories can be explicit (conscious) or implicit (unconscious), and they can influence our decision-making process by serving as a reference for our interpretations and actions in new situations. While experiences are the actual events that occur in our lives, memories are the way we store and recall those events. Experiences help form memories, which then inform our beliefs, mindsets, and emotional responses to new situations. The availability heuristic, a cognitive bias, suggests that people tend to rely on readily available memories when making decisions, which can skew their perception of reality.

In summary, both experiences and memories play a role in shaping our decision-making processes, but they are distinct concepts in the sequence.

Beliefs and Mindsets

Beliefs. Beliefs are the convictions or assumptions we hold about ourselves, others, and the world around us. These beliefs can be based on our experiences, memories, cultural background, or the information we've been exposed to. Beliefs can be both accurate and inaccurate. They play a crucial role in how we perceive and interpret situations and therefore play a critical role in what we decide to do in any given situation.

Beliefs can be divided into different types:

> **Self-beliefs.** These are the beliefs we have about our abilities, character, and worth. Self-esteem, for instance, is a self-belief that influences how we perceive ourselves in relation to others. People with high self-esteem are more likely to interpret negative comments as isolated incidents that don't define their overall worth, whereas those with low self-esteem might internalize the negativity and see it as a confirmation of their perceived inadequacy.

> **Beliefs about others.** These are the assumptions we make about other people's intentions, abilities, and motivations. For example, if we believe someone is trustworthy, we're more likely to interpret their actions positively, while if we think they're deceitful, we might perceive their actions as manipulative or self-serving.

> **Beliefs about the world.** These are our beliefs about how the world functions and the nature of reality. These beliefs can encompass our understanding of societal norms, values, expectations, and broader concepts such as justice, fairness, and morality.

Mindsets. Mindsets refer to the mental attitudes or dispositions that shape our perspective and influence our approach to situations. One of the most widely recognized distinctions in mindset research is between the fixed and growth mindset, popularized by psychologist Carol Dweck.[18]

Fixed mindset

People with fixed mindsets believe their abilities, intelligence, and talents are static and unchangeable. As a result, they often view challenges as threats to their self-image and may avoid them to prevent failure or preserve their perceived competence.

---

[18] Dweck C. S. (2006). *Mindset: The new psychology of success.* Random House.

They are also more likely to give up when faced with obstacles, as they believe their abilities are predetermined and cannot be improved.

Growth mindset

In contrast, individuals with a growth mindset view their abilities, intelligence, and talents as malleable and capable of development through effort and learning. They see each challenge as a "Crisitunity," an opportunity to grow and improve. A growth mindset drives individuals to perseverance, resilience, and adaptability, as people believe they can develop their skills and overcome obstacles with persistence and dedication.

Beliefs and mindsets significantly impact the meaning we assign to situations, which, in turn, influences our emotional responses and decision-making. By understanding how our beliefs and mindsets shape our interpretations, we can work towards cultivating more adaptive and effective decision-making processes.

3. Emotional Signal (How should I feel about this?)
The third step in our cycle occurs once a meaning has been assigned to the trigger. This is when you first experience emotions. This is where we answer the question, either consciously or subconsciously, "How do I feel about this?" Emotions serve as signals that guide our decision-making.

The **Appraisal Theory of Emotion** is a psychological framework that posits emotions are generated by our cognitive appraisal of a situation or event. In other words, emotions arise from the way we interpret and evaluate our experiences. This theory suggests that our emotional responses are not simply automatic reactions to external stimuli but are instead shaped by our perceptions, beliefs, and expectations about the world. In other words, *we do have some control over them*, maybe not at any given time of a trigger, but in shaping them prior to the trigger. Appraisal theorists argue that we assess situations along several dimensions, including their relevance to our goals, the potential consequences, and our ability to cope with or control the situation. These appraisals can occur both consciously and subconsciously, and individual differences, cultural factors, and experiences can influence them. The Appraisal Theory of Emotion helps explain why people react differently to the same event[19]. Because individuals may appraise situations differently based on their unique perspectives and experiences, their emotional responses will also vary accordingly.[20]

4. Reaction Decision: (How should I react?)

Once emotions present themselves, the second decision is made. Remember, the first decision was *what does this stimulus mean?* The next decision is, now that I "know" what it means, h*ow do I react?*

Emotions significantly influence this decision-making process. The **Somatic Marker Hypothesis**[21] posits that emotional responses to certain situations can help guide decision-making regarding how we react, particularly in complex or ambiguous scenarios. Emotions can lead us to make rational or irrational decisions, depending on how well we can regulate and interpret our emotions.

According to this theory, emotional responses trigger physiological changes in one's body, such as changes in heart rate, blood pressure, or skin conductance. These bodily changes create somatic markers that serve as signals or cues that inform the decision-making process. The brain then integrates the somatic markers, either consciously or subconsciously, into the

---

[19] Roseman, I. J. (1984). Cognitive determinants of emotion: A structural theory. In K. R. Scherer & P. Ekman (Eds.), *Approaches to emotion* (pp. 145-166). Erlbaum.

[20] Lazarus, R. S. (1991). Emotion and Adaptation. New York: Oxford University Press

[21] Damasio, A. R. (1994). Descartes' error and the future of human life. *Scientific American*, 271*(4)*, 144-147.

decision-making process. The markers act as a shortcut that allows us to quickly evaluate potential outcomes based on our experiences and emotional responses. They can bias our decisions towards options that have been associated with positive emotions in the past and away from those linked to negative emotions.

The Somatic Marker Hypothesis is used to explain how our reactions to stimuli are shaped by the integration of emotional and physiological information into our decision-making processes. By linking emotions to past experiences and outcomes, somatic markers can guide our decisions and ultimately influence our reactions to specific situations.[22]

5. Response

Once a decision has been made, the individual initiates a response based on that decision. The response is an observable manifestation of the decision that reflects the individual's chosen course of action. It can take various forms, including:

Verbal communication. The response might involve expressing thoughts, feelings, or intentions through spoken or written language. This communication could include offering an opinion, making a request, agreeing or disagreeing with someone, or providing information.

Non-verbal communication. Non-verbal cues, such as facial expressions, body language, gestures, or eye contact, can also convey the individual's response to a situation. These signals often accompany verbal communication, providing others with additional context and meaning.

Physical action. The response can entail engaging in specific behaviors or activities as a result of the decision. For example, this action might involve making

---

[22] Damasio, A. R. (1994). Descartes' error and the future of human life. *Scientific American*, 271 *(4)*, 144-147.

a purchase, starting a new project, changing one's habits, or interacting with others in a particular manner.

Emotional expression. The individual's response may also include displaying emotions such as happiness, sadness, anger, or surprise. These emotional expressions can communicate the individual's feelings and reactions to others, influencing interpersonal dynamics and social interactions.

Cognitive adjustment. In some cases, the response may involve a shift in mental focus or perspective. This shift could include reevaluating beliefs, reassessing goals, or adopting a new mindset as a result of the decision-making process.

Regardless of the response's specific form, it represents the culmination of the decision-making process and serves as an outward expression of the individual's chosen course of action. The response can have various consequences for the individual and others involved in the situation, shaping future experiences, memories, and decisions.

6. Effect (What is the effect?)

The final step in the cause-and-effect process is the effect or outcome that results from the response. The outcome is a consequence of the individual's decision and subsequent actions, and it can have various implications:

Personal impact. The effect may directly influence the individual's life, such as their emotional well-being, relationships, finances, or health. The outcome can be positive or negative, depending on the effectiveness of the decision and response.

Learning and growth. The outcome can provide valuable feedback, allowing the individual to learn from their decisions and refine their decision-making process in the future. In addition, it can contribute to personal growth and development as the individual gains a deeper understanding of the factors that led to the effect and how they might modify their approach in similar situations.

Reinforcement or alteration of beliefs and mindsets. The effect can either reinforce or challenge the individual's existing beliefs and mindsets. Positive outcomes may confirm the validity of their beliefs and mindsets, while negative outcomes may prompt a reevaluation and potential adjustment.

Influence on future emotional responses. The effect can also shape the individual's emotional responses to similar situations in the future. For example, if the outcome is positive, they may be more likely to experience positive emotions in similar contexts, while a negative outcome may increase the likelihood of negative emotions in the future.

Impact on others. The effect may not only impact the individual but also have consequences for others involved in the situation, such as family members, friends, colleagues, or even broader social or environmental systems. These consequences can, in turn, affect the experiences, memories, beliefs, and mindsets of others, influencing their decision-making processes as well.

The effect or outcome is a crucial component of the Emotional Decision Pathway Model ("cause-and-effect process"), as it represents the culmination of the sequence and has implications for both the individual and the wider context.

The Pause and Reflect Strategy: Conscious Intervention

"Between stimulus and response there is a space.
In that space is our power to choose our response.
In our response lies our growth and our freedom."
- Viktor Frankl

There are three opportunities within the cause-and-effect cycle where conscious intervention can take place to mindfully interrupt the cycle and transform the subconscious decisions being made into conscious ones that serve our best interests. The three entry points where this can be done are:

1. Meaning Decision stage.

When an individual attaches meaning to a situation, they can pause to reflect on their interpretations and perceptions. For example, imagine a person receiving constructive criticism from their supervisor. Instead of immediately interpreting the feedback as negative and feeling attacked, they can pause and consider alternative perspectives, such as the possibility that the supervisor is genuinely trying to help them improve. The idea here is to *choose a meaning that serves your best interests.* By becoming more aware of how past experiences, memories, beliefs, and mindsets are influencing their appraisal, they can challenge and reevaluate these factors to make a more informed decision. This conscious intervention promotes rational and beneficial decision-making by choosing a meaning that serves their overall best interests.

2. Emotion Decision stage.

In the Emotion Decision stage, individuals can pause and consciously choose an emotion that serves their best interests. Emotions are signals produced by our brains in response to various internal and external stimuli that guide us in how to react. While they can be helpful in guiding our behavior, they can also lead us astray if we let them control our decision-making. By choosing an emotion that aligns with our goals and values, we can use it as a signal to act or react in a way that serves our overall best interests. This can be done through emotional regulation techniques, such as cognitive reappraisal, which involves reinterpreting a situation (the first stage) to change its emotional impact. By creating a more helpful emotional state, individuals can make clearer more rational decisions that align with their goals and values.

3.   Reaction Decision stage

Once emotions have been elicited, an individual can once again PAUSE to practice emotional regulation techniques to manage their feelings and prevent them from dictating their decision-making. For example, suppose a person feels angry after hearing a controversial political opinion. In that case, they can use the "Arootah" technique my team, and I use to remind ourselves to breathe and calm down before responding. Additionally, individuals can engage in cognitive reappraisal, a process of reinterpreting the situation to change its emotional impact. In this case, they might choose to see the opinion as an opportunity for a productive discussion rather than a personal affront. By doing so, they can create a more balanced emotional state, which will allow them to make clearer, more rational decisions that align with their best interests.

It is possible to mindfully intervene at these three entry points within the cause-and-effect cycle, the Meaning Decision, the Emotional Decision, and the Reaction Decision stages. This serves to interrupt the process and shift subconscious decision-making to more conscious decision-making, whereby you can make rational choices that serve your best interests. In this way, you can become more aware of the factors influencing your perceptions and emotional responses, reevaluate these influences, and engage in emotional regulation techniques. This approach allows for more balanced, rational decision-making and promotes personal growth, emotional resilience, and effective communication in various situations.

The Pause and Reflect Process for Emotional Management

Now, let's put this all together into one process. As a reminder, the three key questions we want to *consciously* answer (i.e., decisions we want to make) when faced with a stimulus (the "cause") are:

1. What does this mean?
2. How should I feel about it?
3. How should I react?

We will want to make these decisions mindfully (with the logical reasoning area of the mind). To do so, we will need to consciously intervene in the Emotional Pathway Model noted above by utilizing the Pause and Reflect Strategy.

1. Cause (Stimulus or Trigger)

The first step in the sequence is the stimulus or trigger. This is the event or situation that **causes** an individual to go through the following steps in the process to decide how to, or if they should, react to this trigger.

2. Meaning Appraisal (What Does This Mean?)

The second step involves attaching *meaning* to the trigger. You are asking yourself, "What does this mean?" In other words, the subconscious mind does an appraisal, recalling experiences and memories and integrating those with beliefs and mindsets to decide what this means. It does this automatically. There is no chance to pause before this meaning is assigned to the stimulus.

3. Pause and Reflect on the *Meaning*

When an individual associates this initial subconscious-driven meaning to a situation, at this stage, if they are mindful, they can consciously intervene to **pause to reflect** on their interpretations and perceptions. Take a breath and/or close your eyes to engage the pre-frontal cortex, the reasoning part of the brain. The idea here is to ask your pre-frontal cortex to *choose a meaning that serves your best interests*. It can be the original meaning if that served your best interests, or it can be a new one if the original did not. Remember that this step moves lightning quick, so if you want a chance to "consciously intervene," you need to *move quickly and train this well.* The idea is to make this a habit. The more times you do it, the easier and faster it will become. However, if you do miss your opportunity, there will be another chance!

4.   Meaning Reframe

This step assumes that you have paused and assigned a new meaning to the situation. A meaning that will serve your best interests. Meanings are the precursor or trigger to the next steps in the process.

5.   Emotional Signal (How Should I Feel?)

Once a meaning has been assigned to the trigger, we experience emotions. This is an automatic process. We don't get to pause here. Emotions serve as signals that guide our decision-making. Remember, emotions are signals to react. So, at this stage, you are getting ready to take action based on the signal of the emotion. If you were successful in pausing and reflecting at the meaning stage, the emotion elicited would likely be the emotion that you needed to achieve the objective that your conscious reasoning mind arrived at. Remember that this may be a positive or negative emotion. Both can serve our objectives.

6.   Pause and Reflect on the *Emotion*

Once the emotional decision has been made, whether or not we have revised the meaning, the emotion itself can serve as another trigger (reminder!) that we have another opportunity to pause and reflect. In other words, they can consciously intervene at this stage to *pause to reflect* on the emotion, and resulting signal, that has been automatically "generated" by the subconscious mind. Similar to the first pause, here you would take a breath and/ or close your eyes to engage the pre-frontal cortex, the reasoning part of the brain. The idea here is to ask your pre-frontal cortex to *choose an emotion that serves your best interests.* It can be the original emotion if that served your best interests, or it can be a new one if the original did not. Remember that this step also moves lightning quick, so if you want a chance to "consciously intervene," you need to **move quickly and train in this as well**. You will also want to make this a mental habit. The more times you do it, the easier and faster it will become. However, if you do miss your opportunity, there will still be another chance! But it will be your last chance.

7. Reaction Decision (How Should I Respond?)

Once emotions present themselves, the second decision is made. Remember, the first decision was *what does this stimulus mean?* The next decision is, now that I "know" what it means, h*ow should I respond to this trigger? How do I react?* The answer to this question should be well-thought-out because it is the one that actually leads to the response. If you screwed up the first two, this is your last chance to get it right! Think forward about what that response will lead to. Keep in mind that every action must have a reaction. This is known as Newton's Third Law of Motion. Ask this question: "What action, in your best judgment, not clouded by emotion, will lead to the reaction that you are seeking that will serve your best interests?" Once you have that answer…

8. Response

Once a decision has been made, the individual initiates a response based on that decision. The response is an observable manifestation of the decision that reflects the individual's chosen course of action. It can take the various forms previously noted, such as verbal or non-verbal communication, physical action, emotional expression, etc.

Regardless of the specific form the response takes, it represents the culmination of the decision-making process and serves as an outward expression of the individual's chosen course of action. The response can have various consequences for the individual and others involved in the situation, shaping future experiences, memories, and decisions.

9. Effect

This step of the cause-and-effect process is the effect or outcome that arises from the response. This outcome is the consequence of an individual's decision and subsequent actions, and it has significant implications that must be considered BEFORE taking action. As previously discussed, the potential effects include personal impact, learning and growth, reinforcement or alteration of beliefs and mindsets, and impacts on others. The effect or outcome is a crucial component of the Emotional Decision Pathway Model as it represents the culmination of the sequence and has implications for both the individual and the wider context.

10. Reflect and Review

The tenth and final step in the cause-and-effect process is to reflect and review the outcome of the response. By understanding the effects of their decisions and responses, individuals can learn, grow, and adapt, continuously refining their decision-making abilities and emotional responses over time. The model provides a detailed account of the intricate relationship between emotions, cognition, and decision-making, which is essential for anyone seeking to improve their decision-making skills. Only by understanding this relationship can one begin to arrive at methods or processes to disrupt or hack it to ensure it works to their benefit, ultimately leading to more effective decision-making and a more fulfilling life. This reflection and review step is critical to understanding the effectiveness of the previous steps in the process and identifying areas for improvement in future decision-making.

Conclusion

Developing greater awareness and control over our emotional responses is essential for making more intentional, logical, and constructive choices. The Pause and Reflect Strategy and emotional regulation techniques, such as cognitive reappraisal, can help us interrupt automatic or habitual thought patterns and behaviors, so we can make more informed and intentional choices. By becoming more aware of how past experiences, memories, beliefs, and mindsets influence our appraisal, we can challenge and reevaluate these factors to make a more informed decision that serves our best interests. Using emotional regulation techniques, we can manage our emotional responses and prevent them from dictating our decision-making. By doing so, we can create a more balanced emotional state, which will allow us to make clearer, more rational decisions that align with our goals and values. Ultimately, developing greater awareness and control over our emotional responses is a process that requires practice and patience, but the benefits are worth it. It can lead to better decision-making, improved relationships, and a more fulfilling life.

Summary

1. Emotions have a powerful impact on the decisions we make.

2. Making decisions based on emotions can lead to poor choices.

3. The Pause and Reflect Strategy helps break the cycle of emotional decision-making.

4. The three pivotal decisions within the "cause-and-effect" cycle are: what does this mean, how should I feel about it, and what should I do about it?

5. Memories, both conscious and unconscious, can influence our decision-making process.

6. Positive emotions can lead to better problem-solving, but negative emotions can lead us astray.

7. Conscious intervention involves intentionally interrupting automatic thought patterns and behaviors.

8. The prefrontal cortex plays a crucial role in assessing whether our emotional responses align with our goals and interests.

9. Emotions can be managed through emotional regulation techniques, such as cognitive reappraisal.

10. By utilizing the Pause and Reflect Strategy, we can improve our decision-making abilities and avoid making impulsive or regretful decisions.

Questions

1. What is the Pause and Reflect Strategy?

    Taking a moment to step back when a trigger arises and then
    reflecting before making a decision.

2. How can emotions impact our decision-making?

    They can cloud our judgment and cause us to focus on short-
    term gains.

3. What is a conscious intervention?

    The intentional and deliberate effort to interrupt automatic or
    habitual thought patterns and behaviors.

4. How can memories influence our decision-making?

    They serve as a reference for our interpretations and actions in
    new situations.

5. What are the three pivotal decisions within the "cause-and-
    effect" cycle?

    What does this mean? How should I feel? What should I do?

6. Can positive emotions lead us astray?

    They can cause us to be overconfident or optimistic.

7. What is emotional regulation?

    Managing and modifying one's emotions.

8. How can the "Pause and Reflect" Strategy help us make better
    decisions?

    It can help break the cycle of emotional decision-making.

9. What is cognitive reappraisal?

    An emotional regulation technique that involves reinterpreting
    a situation to change its emotional impact.

10. How can conscious intervention promote rational decision-
    making?

    By choosing a meaning that serves our overall best interests.

Exercises

1. Set your intention to take the positive mental diet challenge for ten days. During the challenge, make a conscious effort to become aware whenever you slip into a negative mindset or take part in negative self-talk.

2. Practice the Pause and Reflect strategy whenever you feel triggered by a situation or decision. Take a moment to step back, reflect, and consciously choose a response that aligns with your values and goals.

3. Identify the situations or people that trigger negative emotions and responses in you. Then, write them down and reflect on ways to reframe or re-interpret these triggers in a more positive light.

4. Keep a daily gratitude journal for the challenge, listing three things you are grateful for each day. This practice can help cultivate a more positive and optimistic outlook on life.

5. Practice cognitive reappraisal, which involves reinterpreting a situation to change its emotional impact. For example, if you receive constructive criticism, try to view it as an opportunity for growth and improvement rather than a personal attack.

6. Practice mindful breathing whenever you feel overwhelmed or stressed. Take a few deep breaths, focusing on the sensations in your body and letting go of any negative thoughts or emotions.

7. Eliminate negative self-talk by consciously choosing positive thoughts and affirmations. For example, replace "I can't do this" with "I am capable and will give it my best effort."

8. Visualize yourself succeeding and achieving your goals every day during the mental diet challenge. Use this visualization as motivation to take proactive steps toward your goals.

9. Practice emotion regulation techniques, such as deep breathing or progressive muscle relaxation, to manage negative emotions and prevent them from impacting your decision-making.

10. Practice mindfulness by focusing on the present moment and letting go of worries about the future or regrets about the past.

Principle 5

Intervene Consciously to Break the Habit Cycle

*"Your net worth to the world is usually
determined by what remains after your bad habits
are subtracted from your good ones."*

- Benjamin Franklin

Utilizing the Pause and Seize Strategy to Instill and Break Habits

Cultivating positive habits involves intentionally developing positive behaviors through mindful awareness and conscious intervention. By reshaping thought patterns and actively focusing on positive habits, you can improve your decision-making abilities and achieve greater success. This principle underscores the significance of deliberately creating positive change and taking action to achieve desired outcomes. By intentionally cultivating positive habits, you can have a more positive impact on your decision-making abilities, ultimately leading to greater success and fulfillment.

Key Question
How can we utilize a Pause and Seize strategy to break automatic patterns of behavior that result in bad habits and intervene with conscious decision-making to cultivate positive habits?

Have you ever felt like your habits were out of your control or like they were just something that happened automatically without you even thinking about them? It's easy to fall into this mindset, but the truth is that habits are not set in stone. In fact, habits are decisions – conscious or unconscious – that we make every day.

A study by Duke University found that up to 45% of our daily behavior is habitual, meaning that we do it without conscious thought or decision-making.[23]

The good news is that because habits involve decisions to act, we have the power to intervene and consciously shape them. By recognizing the power of our decisions in habit formation, we can develop positive habits that align with our goals and values and break negative ones that hold us back.

In this chapter, we will explore the principle that "Habits are Decisions" and discover how we can use conscious decision-making to interrupt automatic patterns of behavior and create new, intentional habits. Finally, we'll discuss the role of mindfulness and self-awareness in recognizing automatic patterns and bring back our reliable old friend, the Pause and Reflect Strategy, to provide us with a process to break free from negative habitual behaviors.

By the end of this chapter, you'll have a deeper understanding of the power of conscious decision-making in shaping our habits as well as the tools you need to cultivate positive habits that align with your goals and values and break those that don't.

Habits Are Decisions!

Understanding the nature of habits and how they relate to decision-making is crucial for developing positive habits and breaking negative ones. Habits can be defined as automatic, unconscious behaviors that we repeat in response to certain cues or triggers. They are formed through repetition when our brains

---

[23] Wood, W., Neal, D. T., & Quinn, J. M. (2019). Habits in everyday life: Thought, emotion, and action. *Journal of Personality and Social Psychology*, 117*(6)*, 1110–1129.

learn to associate a particular behavior with a specific context or situation.

Contrary to popular belief, habits do, in fact, provide us with the opportunity for choice – whether conscious or unconscious – to engage in a particular behavior. Each time we engage in a behavior, we reinforce the neural pathways associated with that behavior, increasing the probability of automatic repetition in the future and reducing the likelihood of making a conscious choice without considerable effort.

Automaticity

One of the key features of habits is **automaticity**, or the tendency to engage in a behavior without conscious thought. This is due to the role of *habit loops*, which are a sequence of three components: a cue or *trigger*, a routine *behavior*, and a *reward*. Over time, the brain learns to associate the cue with the routine behavior and the reward, creating a cycle of automaticity that can be difficult to break.

Here are examples of a positive habit and a negative habit, with their respective cue, routine behavior, and reward:

Positive Habit:

- **Cue:** Waking up in the morning
- **Routine behavior:** Going for a morning walk or jog
- **Reward:** Feeling energized and refreshed for the day ahead

Negative Habit:

- **Cue:** Feeling stressed at work
- **Routine behavior:** Snacking on unhealthy foods
- **Reward:** Temporary relief from stress and anxiety

In both examples, the habit loop involves a cue, routine behavior, and reward. For example, the positive habit of going for a morning walk or jog provides us with a reward of energy and revitalization for the day ahead, which reinforces routine behavior and makes it more likely to be repeated in the future. Similarly, the negative habit of snacking on unhealthy foods in response to stress provides temporary relief from stress and anxiety, reinforcing the behavior and making it more likely to be repeated in the future. The power of habit loops and automaticity is why breaking negative habits and developing positive ones can be difficult.

Conscious Intervention

The good news is that **conscious intervention** can play a powerful role in both habit formation and breaking bad habits. By recognizing the power of our decisions in shaping our habits, we can intentionally intervene in the habit loop and replace negative behaviors with positive ones. Through conscious intervention and repetition, we can develop new, intentional habits that align with our goals and values and break free from negative habits that hold us back.

As a reminder, conscious intervention means making an intentional decision to break automatic behavior patterns and make more mindful choices. This requires cultivating self-awareness and recognizing when we are operating on autopilot. By interrupting the cycle of automaticity, we can create space for conscious intervention and make intentional decisions about our habits.

Consulting Your Future Self: Guiding Habit Formation with Long-Term Insight

Our actions today have a significant impact on our future selves. When faced with decisions or tempted by bad habits, it's essential to consider how our choices will affect us in the long run. One powerful technique to promote positive habit formation is to consult with your future self, envisioning the person you aspire to become and seeking guidance from that imagined perspective.

The process of consulting your future self can be broken down into the following steps:

1. *Visualize your future self:* Close your eyes and imagine yourself in the future. Consider the values, habits, and mindset that have contributed to your success.
2. *Identify the decision or habit:* Clearly define the decision you are facing or the habit you are tempted to indulge in.
3. *Consult your future self:* Ask your future self for guidance on how to approach the situation. For example, would your future self encourage you to indulge in the bad habit, or would they advise against it? What alternative actions might your future self suggest that align better with your long-term goals?
4. *Reflect on the guidance:* Contemplate the advice you've received from your future self and consider how it aligns with your goals and values.
5. *Make a conscious decision:* Based on the insight from your future self, make a conscious decision to either resist the bad habit or engage in a more positive behavior that supports your long-term aspirations.

By consulting your future self, you connect your present actions to your long-term goals and reinforce the importance of making choices that contribute to your overall well-being and success. This approach encourages you to prioritize your future self's needs over immediate gratification, empowering you to

Habit Strategies

Developing effective strategies to break bad habits and instill good ones can be transformative, paving the way for a more fulfilling and productive life. In this section, we will explore two powerful habit strategies: the Pause and Reflect Strategy, designed to help break negative habits, and the Seize the Moment Strategy, aimed at fostering positive habits. By understanding and applying these strategies, you can harness the power of conscious decision-making to create lasting, positive changes in your life.

The "Pause and Reflect" Strategy for Breaking Negative Habits

The **"Pause and Reflect" Strategy** is a simple but powerful framework for interrupting automatic behavior patterns and creating space for conscious decision-making. For example, when we feel the urge to engage in a negative habit, we can take a moment to pause, reflect, and choose a different path. There are many benefits of pausing before making a decision or engaging in a habit.

For instance, let's go back to the habit of mindlessly snacking whenever you feel stressed or bored. This habit has resulted in weight gain and a lack of control over your eating habits. In this situation, you can consciously intervene the next time you get that urge by utilizing the "Pause and Reflect" strategy. Pause and reflect *before* making a decision to reach for that bag of chips. You can ask yourself, "Why am I feeling the urge to snack? Am I really hungry, or am I just bored or stressed? What is my objective here?" By bringing greater awareness to your habit, you can begin to make intentional decisions about your behavior.

There are several books and references that discuss the power of the "Pause and Reflect" strategy in breaking negative habits and making conscious decisions. For example, Charles Duhigg's book *The Power of Habit*[24] delves into the science behind habit formation and how we can use conscious intervention to break automatic behavior patterns. Additionally, there are many movie references that illustrate the power of conscious decision-making and the importance of breaking negative habits. For example, in the movie *Limitless*,[25] the main character uses a pill to enhance his brain function and becomes addicted to the drug.

---

[24] The Power of Habit: Why We Do What We Do in Life and Business by Charles Duhigg was published by Random House in 2012.

[25] "Limitless" is a 2011 American science fiction thriller film directed by Neil Burger and starring Bradley Cooper, Robert De Niro, and Abbie Cornish.

However, he is eventually able to break the cycle of addiction by consciously making the decision to stop taking the pill and take control of his life.

The "Pause and Reflect" Process

1. **Recognize the BAD habit.** Identify the habit you want to break and the trigger or cue that sets off the habit loop.
2. **Pause.** When you feel the urge to engage in the habit, take a moment to pause and take a few deep breaths.
3. **Reflect.** Reflect on your thoughts, feelings, and intentions. Ask yourself why you are engaging in this habit and whether it aligns with your goals and values.
4. **Choose a different path.** Based on your reflection, choose a different path if necessary. Make a conscious decision to break the cycle of automaticity and create a new habit or behavior that aligns with your goals and values.

Example: The "Pause and Reflect" Process

Let's say you have a habit of mindlessly scrolling through social media whenever you feel bored or anxious. You notice that this habit consumes a lot of your time and prevents you from being productive. The next time you feel the urge to scroll through social media, you can pause and reflect before making a decision. You can ask yourself, "Why am I feeling the urge to check social media? Am I really bored or anxious, or am I just avoiding a task I need to do? What would be a more productive use of my time?" By bringing greater awareness to your habit, you can begin to make intentional decisions about your behavior.

The "Seize the Moment" Strategy for Instilling Positive Habits

The **Seize the Moment Strategy** is a powerful framework for instilling positive habits. It involves taking action within a few seconds of getting the idea to do something positive that will lead to a good habit if done over time. The key is to take this action *before our minds talk us out of it*. By seizing the moment, we interrupt the cycle of automaticity and create space for conscious intervention, allowing us to make intentional decisions about cultivating new positive habits.

Our minds often come up with reasons why we shouldn't exercise, even if we know it's good for us. In fact, our brains are wired to *conserve energy* and avoid exertion whenever possible. When we wake up in the morning with the idea to go for a run, our minds may immediately come up with reasons why it's not a good idea, such as "I'm too tired," "It's too cold outside," and "I don't have enough time." These thoughts can quickly turn into automatic patterns of behavior that prevent us from taking action.

To interrupt this line of thinking and take action, we can utilize the Seize strategy. By immediately putting on our workout clothes and heading out the door within a few seconds of getting the idea to go for a run, we can break free from automatic patterns and create space for conscious decision-making. This space allows us to reflect on our thoughts, feelings, and intentions and make conscious decisions about our behavior.

One way to counterbalance the intrinsic wiring of our brains is to create a plan. For example, we can lay out our workout clothes the night before, choose a running route ahead of time, and set a specific time to go for a run. By having a plan in place, we can reduce the mental effort required to take action and make it easier to follow through with our intentions. This is setting us up for success, which we will discuss in more depth when we get to Principle 11.

Another way to interrupt negative patterns of thinking is to use positive affirmations. When we catch ourselves thinking negatively, we can replace those thoughts with positive affirmations such as "I am strong and capable," "I am committed to my health and well-being," or "I am making progress towards my goals." This helps to reframe our thoughts in a positive light and shift our mindset, allowing us to make more conscious decisions.

The 5 Second Rule

The *5 Second Rule* by Mel Robbins[26] is a book about taking action and overcoming procrastination. In the book, Robbins explains that our minds are wired to protect us from uncertainty and risk, which often leads to inaction and procrastination. The **5 Second Rule** is a technique that helps us to take action before our minds talk us out of it.

The story of the 5 Second Rule that Mel Robbins shares in her book is based on a scene from the movie *Jerry Maguire*.[27] In the movie, the main character, played by Tom Cruise, has a sudden urge to tell his love interest, played by Renée Zellweger, how he feels about her. So he counts down from five and then blurts out his feelings before his mind has a chance to talk him out of it. Mel Robbins uses this scene as an example of how the 5 Second Rule can be applied to real-life situations and help us to take action before our minds talk us out of it.

The rule is simple: *When you have an idea or urge to do something that aligns with your goals and values (like a habit you are trying to instill), count down from five and take action.* Counting creates a small amount of stress that interrupts the automatic patterns of behavior in our minds and allows us to act with more intention and consciousness.

In the context of instilling positive habits, the 5 Second Rule can be a powerful tool for acting quickly and interrupting the cycle of automaticity. When we have an idea or urge to engage in a positive habit such as exercise, we can use the 5 Second Rule to interrupt the automatic cycle of behavior in our minds, allowing us to make more intentional decisions that align with our values and aspirations. This can help us establish new, positive patterns of behavior that support our goals and values.

---

[26] Robbins, M. (2017). The 5 Second Rule: Transform Your Life, Work, and Confidence with Everyday Courage. Savio Republic.

[27] Crowe, C. (Director). (1996). Jerry Maguire [Motion picture]. United States: TriStar Pictures.

The "Seize the Moment" Strategy

1. **Recognize the GOOD habit.** Identify the habit you want to cultivate and the trigger or cue that sets off the habit loop.
2. **Seize the moment.** When you get the idea to engage in the habit, act quickly (within a few seconds). Take immediate action to reinforce the behavior *before* the mind leads you elsewhere.
3. **Repeat the behavior.** Repeat the behavior consistently over time to reinforce the habit loop and create a new automatic pattern of behavior.

Example: The "Seize the Moment" Process

Let's say you want to instill a morning exercise habit. Whenever you wake up in the morning, you have the idea to go for a run. By utilizing the "Seize the Moment" strategy, you can immediately put on your workout clothes and head out the door within a few seconds of getting the idea. By acting quickly, you interrupt the cycle of automaticity and create space for conscious intervention. This space allows you to reflect on your thoughts, feelings, and intentions and to make conscious decisions about your behavior.

These examples illustrate how the "Pause and Reflect" and "Seize the Moment" strategies can be applied to specific habits, providing a framework for making conscious decisions about our behavior.

Conclusion

Developing positive habits requires intentional decision-making and the cultivation of self-awareness. By recognizing the power of our decisions in shaping our habits, we can interrupt automatic behavior patterns and create new, intentional habits that align with our goals and values. The Pause and Seize strategies provide powerful tools for breaking free from negative habits and instilling positive ones. Through conscious intervention and repetition, we can develop new habits that improve our decision-making abilities, leading to greater success and fulfillment. Ultimately, by taking control of our habits, we can achieve our goals and live a more fulfilling life.

Summary
1. Habits are not set in stone and involve conscious or unconscious decisions that we make every day.
2. We can consciously intervene and shape our habits by recognizing the power of our decisions in habit formation.
3. The automaticity of habits can be difficult to break because of the habit loops that involve a cue, routine behavior, and reward.
4. Conscious intervention can help in developing positive habits and breaking negative ones.
5. The Pause and Reflect Strategy is a powerful tool for interrupting automatic patterns of behavior and creating space for conscious decision-making.
6. Pausing allows us to interrupt the cycle of automaticity and reflect on our thoughts, feelings, and intentions.
7. Mindfulness and self-awareness play a crucial role in helping us recognize automatic patterns and develop positive habits.
8. Positive habits align with our goals and values, while negative habits hold us back.
9. We reinforce neural pathways associated with a particular behavior each time we engage in that behavior.
10. By cultivating positive habits, we can increase our net worth to the world by subtracting our bad habits.

Questions

1. What are habits?

    They are automatic, unconscious behaviors.

2. Can we consciously shape our habits?

    We need to recognize the power of our decisions.

3. Why is automaticity a key feature of habits?

    It is the tendency to engage in behaviors without thought.

4. What is the habit loop?

    A neurological pattern that has three elements: a cue, routine, and reward.

5. Can mindfulness help us develop positive habits?

    In recognizing automatic patterns, interrupting the cycle of automaticity.

6. How does the Pause and Reflect Strategy help break negative habits?

    It is a tool for interrupting automatic behavior patterns and creating space for conscious decision-making.

7. How can we cultivate self-awareness?

    Being cognizant of our thoughts, emotions, and behaviors without judgment or distraction.

8. How can conscious intervention help with habit formation?

    By intentionally repeating a new behavior that aligns with our values.

9. What is the role of repetition in habit formation?

    It helps us to strengthen the neural pathways.

10. What is the relationship between positive habits and our net worth to the world?

    Positive habits enable us to contribute more effectively to our personal and professional relationships.

Exercises

1. Take a few minutes to reflect on one of your negative habits and write down the triggers that usually lead you to engage in this behavior.

2. Develop a plan for interrupting your negative habit when you feel triggered. This can involve taking a deep breath, using a mantra or visual cue, or engaging in a different activity.

3. Practice pausing and reflecting on your negative habit several times a day for a week, and note any changes in your behavior or thought patterns.

4. Identify a positive habit you want to develop and write down the specific actions you can take to make it a part of your daily routine.

5. Set a goal to act on your positive habit within five seconds of getting the idea to do so, and track your progress over the course of a week or month.

6. Create a visual reminder of your positive habit, such as a sticky note on your computer or a picture on your phone, to help keep it top of mind.

7. Find an accountability partner who can help you stay on track with your habit goals and check in with them regularly to share your progress and challenges.

8. Consider using a habit-tracking app to help you monitor your progress and stay motivated.

9. Reward yourself for sticking to your positive habit, whether with a small treat or by engaging in a favorite activity.

10. Reflect on what you've learned from this exercise and use this insight to continue developing positive habits and breaking negative ones in the future.

Principle 6

Adopt a Proven Framework

"If you can't describe what you are doing as a process, you don't know what you are doing."

— W. Edwards Deming

Navigating Complex Issues with a Structured Approach

Adopting a proven systematic strategy emphasizes the importance of using a structured approach to decision-making, including gathering information, evaluating options, considering risks, and identifying potential outcomes. Following a systematic approach can reduce the risk of errors and help you make more informed and effective decisions. Adopting a proven systematic strategy for decision-making is crucial as it helps you base decisions on facts and evidence rather than intuition or emotions, resulting in more successful outcomes. This principle highlights the significance of a clear and structured decision-making process to ensure optimal results.

Key Question

What is a proven framework for making effective strategic decisions, and how can adopting such a framework help to reduce errors and lead to more successful outcomes?

There are two types of *conscious* decisions: *urgent* and *strategic*. Urgent decisions require a quick response to prevent harm or mitigate risks. Examples of urgent decisions include responding to emergencies, addressing customer complaints, resolving a production or supply chain issue, and dealing with legal or compliance issues.

The second type of a decision, **strategic decisions**, are those that can be made over a longer period of time and do not require an immediate response or action. These decisions often involve complex or strategic issues that require careful consideration and analysis. Examples of strategic decisions include long-term strategic planning, investment decisions, hiring or staffing decisions, and major capital expenditures.

In this chapter, we will discuss a *framework* for making strategic decisions. Because urgent decisions require an immediate response, there may not be time for extensive analysis or consideration of multiple options; decision-makers must rely on their judgment and experience to make the best decision possible with the available information. While urgent decisions may be stressful and require quick thinking, they are necessary for any business or organization. By responding quickly and decisively to urgent situations, businesses can minimize the impact of unforeseen events and ensure they can continue operating effectively.

Taking the time to deliberate and carefully consider strategic decisions can help you ensure that you are making the right decision and that the decision aligns with the overall goals and objectives of your business or organization. According to research on decision-making, time pressure, and stress, people tend to make better decisions when they have more information and more time to consider their options. Moreover, participants who are given more time to make decisions tended to make choices that are more aligned with their long-term goals.[28] By contrast, making a hasty decision without proper analysis or consideration can lead to unintended consequences and potentially negative outcomes. Another study published in the *Journal of Defense Resources Management* found that individuals who made quick decisions tended to experience more regret than those who took more time to make decisions and that people

---

[28] Svenson, O., & Maule, A. J. (Eds.) (1993). *Time pressure and stress in human judgment and decision making.* Plenum.

who made hasty decisions were more likely to experience regret, even when their decisions turned out well.[29]

Importance of Process

While some people may seem to have a natural talent for making good decisions, the truth is that *anyone* can improve their decision-making skills by creating and following a *decision-making process*. In fact, having a decision-making process is crucial to making quality decisions, especially when dealing with complex situations. By breaking down complex issues into simple steps, a decision-making process can help us make more informed and effective decisions, leading to better outcomes and greater success. The key benefits of having a repeatable process are many, but here are just a few.

Consistency. A consistent decision-making process ensures that all decisions are made using the same criteria and considerations to reduce the risk of bias or errors.

A hiring manager can use a consistent process to evaluate job candidates using the same criteria to ensure the best candidate is selected. At Arootah, this is a cornerstone of our Talent Acquisition Process. We score each candidate based on carefully chosen and weighted criteria.

Efficiency. An efficient decision-making process ensures that decisions are made in a timely manner, reducing the risk of missed opportunities or delays.

A project manager can use an efficient process for making decisions about project timelines and resource allocation, ensuring that projects are completed on time and within budget.

---

[29] Vasilescu, C. (2011). Effective strategic decision making. *Journal of Defense Resources Management (JoDRM), 2(1)*, 101-106.

Accountability. A decision-making process that assigns specific responsibilities and roles ensures that individuals are held accountable for their decisions and actions.

A financial advisor can use a process to document investment decisions and ensure that they are aligned with the client's goals and risk tolerance.

Quality Control. A decision-making process that includes quality control measures ensures that decisions are based on accurate and reliable information.

A marketing manager can use a process to gather customer feedback and ensure that decisions about product features or marketing campaigns are informed by that feedback.

Continuous Improvement. A decision-making process that includes evaluation and feedback mechanisms ensures that decisions are continuously improved over time.

A product development team can use a process for testing and gathering user feedback to make iterative improvements to a product, leading to better customer satisfaction and sales.

Delegation. A decision-making process that is well-documented and clearly defined allows for the effective delegation of decision-making authority.

A team leader can delegate decision-making authority to team members closest to the issue at hand, ensuring that decisions are made quickly and efficiently.

Scalability. A decision-making process designed to handle different levels of complexity and demand ensures that decisions can be made effectively in various situations.

A supply chain manager can use a process to manage disruptions to the supply chain caused by weather events or other unexpected events, ensuring that decisions are made quickly and effectively.

Risk Management. A decision-making process that includes risk assessment and mitigation ensures that decisions are made with an understanding of the potential risks involved.

A business owner can use a process for assessing the risks of expanding into a new market, ensuring that decisions are informed by a comprehensive understanding of the risks and rewards involved.

Training. A decision-making process that is well-documented and clearly defined allows for the effective training of new decision-makers.

A customer service manager can use a process to train new hires on how to handle different types of customer inquiries, ensuring that decisions are made consistently and effectively.

Collaboration. A decision-making process that includes input from multiple stakeholders and encourages collaboration ensures that decisions are informed by a diversity of perspectives and expertise.

A product development team can use a process that includes input from marketing, engineering, and design teams to make decisions about new product features, ensuring that the final product meets the needs and expectations of customers.

10 Step Decision Analysis Framework for Strategic Decisions

Embarking on the journey of making strategic decisions can be daunting but fear not! We have carefully crafted a systematic framework designed to guide you through each step, ensuring you make informed and impactful choices. Let's dive into this comprehensive method and unlock the secrets to mastering the art of strategic decision-making.

1. Define the Right Objective for Effective Decision-Making

Establishing a clear and well-defined objective as the foundation of the decision-making process is critically important. Often, people overlook this step, which can lead to confusion, misaligned priorities, and, ultimately, less-than-optimal decisions. To avoid these pitfalls, it's essential to ask the right questions from the very beginning. Ask the following key question and sub-questions:

Key Question
What is the main goal we want to accomplish with this decision?

---

1. **Core Issue.** What is the underlying problem or opportunity that will require you to make a decision? Be specific and focus on the root cause rather than symptoms or side effects.
2. **Vision.** What does success look like in this scenario? Visualize the ideal end result and consider the short-term and long-term implications of your decision.
3. **Achievable.** What is achievable given the constraints and resources available to you? Balance ambition with feasibility to ensure your objectives are grounded in reality. Be sure that your expectations are reasonable.
4. **Values Alignment.** How does this decision align with your values or the values of your organization? Consider the ethical, moral, and social implications of your decision to ensure they are congruent with your guiding principles.
5. **Measurement.** How will you know if your decision has led to a successful outcome? Develop quantifiable goals or performance indicators to track progress and evaluate the effectiveness of your decision.

By taking the time to ask these pertinent questions and accurately define the objective of your decision, you lay the groundwork for a well-informed and impactful decision-making process. This clarity will not only guide you in your decision-making journey but also ensure that the choices you make are in line with your values and priorities, ultimately leading to better outcomes.

If an individual were purchasing a home in a suburban neighborhood, for example, here's how one could answer the KEY QUESTION, "What is the main goal I want to accomplish with this decision?" in order to define the objective of the decision. Remember, the objective should be a clear and specific statement of what you want to achieve with your decision. In this case, the objective could be "To purchase a home in a suburban neighborhood that meets our needs, preferences, and budget."

2. Understand the Purpose Behind Your Decision for Long-Term Success and Intrinsic Motivation

Once you have defined a clear and well-defined objective, it's essential to understand the underlying purpose or motivation behind it. This step ensures that your decision aligns with your personal or organizational values and contributes to your long-term goals and vision. Understanding the purpose behind your decision will help you to remain adaptable and resilient in the face of challenges. Incorporating the purpose into the decision-making process helps you set the right objectives and provides the inspiration and motivation needed to pursue them. This clarity will keep you focused on your purpose, allowing you to overcome obstacles and maintain your motivation. To clarify the purpose of your decision, ask yourself the following key question and sub-questions:

Key Question
Why is this objective important to us, and how
does it align with our personal or organizational
values?

---

1. **Personal Significance.** What personal factors or emotions are driving your decision? Reflect on your emotional attachment to the objective and how it relates to your personal values, aspirations, or experiences.

2. **Intrinsic Motivation.** What intrinsic motivators, such as personal growth, learning, or fulfillment, are driving your decision? Focusing on these factors can lead you toward more meaningful and sustainable motivation, helping you achieve your objective and remain in alignment with your purpose.

3. **Impact on Others.** How will your decision impact the people around you, such as your family, friends, colleagues, or community? Consider the potential benefits and drawbacks for those affected by your decision.

4. **Long-term Vision.** How does this decision fit into your long-term goals and vision for your life or organization? Ensure that the decision contributes to your overall objectives and doesn't conflict with other priorities.

5. **Sustainability and Adaptability.** Is the decision sustainable over time? Assess the long-term viability of the decision, taking into account potential changes in circumstances, resources, or priorities. Consider whether the decision allows for flexibility and the ability to pivot, if necessary, based on changing conditions or new information.

By exploring these questions, you gain a deeper understanding of the purpose behind your decision and can better align it with your values and long-term vision. This clarity will help you stay focused on what truly matters, make choices that contribute to lasting success and inspire you to keep moving forward toward your objective despite the inevitable obstacles that will present themselves along the way.

Returning to the example of purchasing a home in a suburban neighborhood, let's apply the KEY QUESTION: "Why is this objective important to me, and how does it align with my personal and/or organizational values?" to understand the purpose of the decision. In this case, the purpose could be "To provide a safe, comfortable, and nurturing environment for our family to grow and thrive while maintaining financial stability, work-life balance, and personal growth."

3. Establish Comprehensive Criteria for Effective Decision-Making

Once you have defined a clear objective and understood its underlying purpose, the next step is to identify the specific criteria that will help you evaluate the available options. Establishing a comprehensive set of criteria ensures that your decision-making process is systematic and well-structured, allowing you to make the most informed choice. To determine the most important factors you should consider in the decision-making process to achieve your objective and fulfill your purpose, ask yourself the following key question and sub-questions:

Key Question
What are the most important factors that we need to consider in order to achieve my objective and fulfill my purpose?

---

1. **Relevance.** What factors are most relevant to my objective and purpose?
2. **Comprehensiveness.** Have I considered all aspects of the decision that are important to me, such as financial, emotional, social, and environmental factors?
3. **Consistency.** Are the criteria I've chosen consistent with the objective and purpose I've identified?
4. **Trade-offs.** Am I prepared to make trade-offs between different criteria if necessary? What compromises am I willing to accept to achieve my objective and fulfill my purpose?
5. **Clarity.** Are the criteria I have identified clear and specific enough to be helpful in evaluating my options? Can I effectively measure or assess these criteria?

Based on the example of purchasing a home in a suburban neighborhood, you might ask yourself the following questions to establish criteria:

1. **Price:** Does the home fit within your budget?
2. **Location:** Is the home in a desirable neighborhood or close to amenities, schools, and transportation?
3. **Size:** Does the home have enough bedrooms and living space to accommodate your family's needs?
4. **Layout:** Is the floor plan suitable for your lifestyle and preferences?
5. **Nice kitchen:** Does the home have an updated, functional, and attractive kitchen?
6. **Big backyard:** Is the backyard spacious and suitable for outdoor activities, gardening, or entertaining?
7. **School district:** Are the local schools highly rated and suitable for your children's needs?
8. **Safety and crime rate:** Is the neighborhood safe with low crime rates?

9. **Property condition:** Is the home in good condition, or will it require significant repairs or upgrades?

10. **Potential for appreciation:** Does the home have the potential to increase in value over time?

4. Examine Your Criteria for any Hidden Assumptions and Challenge Their Validity

Reviewing and challenging assumptions is an essential step in the multi-criteria decision-making process. It involves examining the criteria that have been established to evaluate the options and looking for any hidden assumptions that may be influencing the evaluation. These assumptions can often be rooted in past experiences, cultural norms, or personal biases, and they can significantly impact the outcome of the decision-making process.

This step is different from rooting out cognitive biases (our next step) because it focuses specifically on assumptions related to the criteria rather than individual biases affecting the decision-maker. The goal during this step of the process is to ensure that the criteria used to evaluate the options are valid, relevant, and appropriate for the specific problem or decision at hand.

This step can often lead decision-makers to refine the criteria or find alternative solutions. For example, if an assumption is found to be invalid or irrelevant, the criteria may need to be adjusted or replaced with a more appropriate criterion. Similarly, if a decision-maker determines an assumption limits the evaluation of the options, they may need to consider alternative solutions or criteria.

In summary, reviewing and challenging assumptions is an important step in the multi-criteria decision-making process that can help decision-makers ensure that the criteria used to evaluate the options are valid, relevant, and appropriate.

Examples of incorrect assumptions in decision-making include:

- Assuming that Price is a criterion when you know you can only afford a certain amount. In this situation, price is more of a "gating factor" than a criterion and shouldn't even be factored into the decision-making process.
- Assuming that a particular option is the most cost-effective without considering other factors, such as quality, reliability, or maintenance costs.
- Assuming that a particular option is the most sustainable without considering the environmental impact of production, transportation, or disposal.
- Assuming that a particular option is the safest without considering the potential health risks or safety hazards associated with its use.
- Assuming that a particular option is the most convenient without considering the time and effort required to implement and maintain it.
- Assuming that a particular option is the most preferred by customers without considering the preferences of different customer segments or the changing needs and preferences within the market.
- Assuming that a particular option is the most ethical without considering the social and cultural implications of its use or the impact it may have on stakeholders.
- Assuming that a particular option is the most technologically advanced without considering the practicality, feasibility, or reliability of the technology.

- These examples illustrate how incorrect assumptions can lead to suboptimal decisions and demonstrate the importance of challenging assumptions and considering all relevant criteria when making multi-criteria decisions.

A 10-Step Process to Challenge and Uncover Incorrect Assumptions

Here is a 10-step process in priority order that can be used to challenge and uncover incorrect assumptions. Underneath each step, I include an example from the home purchasing decision.

1. Identify Potential Assumptions

Start by identifying the assumptions that may be influencing your decision-making process. This identification may involve reviewing the criteria that have been established or considering the experiences and biases that may be affecting your judgment.

The decision maker may identify assumptions related to the criteria used to evaluate the options, such as assuming that a particular neighborhood is safe because of its high property value, without considering the crime rates.

2. Gather Information

Collect data and information that can help to validate or invalidate the assumptions. This may involve conducting research, consulting with experts, or gathering feedback from stakeholders.

The decision maker can gather data and information on crime rates in the neighborhood, the safety of the area, and the opinions of other residents or real estate agents.

3. Seek Alternative Perspectives

Seek opinions and perspectives from people with different experiences, backgrounds, or expertise. This can help to challenge and broaden your thinking.

The decision maker can seek opinions and perspectives from people who have lived in different neighborhoods or have experience with home buying.

4. Consider the Implications

Consider the implications of the assumptions and what would happen if they were incorrect. This can help to identify any potential risks or unintended consequences.

The decision maker can consider the implications of choosing a home in a neighborhood with high crime rates, such as potential safety hazards or decreased property values.

5. Test the Assumptions.

Test the assumptions by conducting experiments, simulations, or other forms of validation. This can help to determine their validity and reliability.

The decision maker can conduct research or speak to law enforcement officials to determine the crime rates in the area.

6. Reframe the Problem

Reframe the problem or decision to consider alternative perspectives and perspectives. This can help to identify new and creative solutions.

The decision maker can reframe the problem by considering alternative neighborhoods or criteria, such as safety and crime rates, to determine the best option.

7. Consider Counterevidence

Consider the evidence that ***contradicts*** the assumptions and weigh it against the evidence that supports the assumptions.

The decision maker can consider evidence that contradicts the assumption that there is a relationship between the high property value and neighborhood safety, such as data on crime rates in the area.

8. Question the Status Quo

Challenge the status quo by considering alternative approaches and breaking out of established thinking patterns.

The decision maker can challenge the status quo by considering alternative options, such as choosing a home in a safer neighborhood with lower property values.

9. Seek out Dissenting Opinions

Seek out dissenting opinions and engage in constructive dialogue with those who have different perspectives.

The decision maker can seek dissenting opinions from friends, family, or real estate agents who may have different perspectives on the neighborhood's safety.

10. Re-evaluate the Criteria

Re-evaluate the criteria used to make the decision and consider alternative criteria that may be more relevant or appropriate.

The decision maker can re-evaluate the criteria used to make the decision, such as considering safety and crime rates as a more important factor than property value.

By following this process, you can challenge and uncover incorrect assumptions and improve the quality and accuracy of your decision-making. It's important to be open-minded, flexible, and willing to change your thinking as new information becomes available.

5. Uncover Cognitive Biases

Be aware of potential cognitive biases that may influence your decision-making. In a multi-criteria decision-making process, it is important to review and challenge any cognitive biases that may be influencing your evaluation of options. This step involves examining the criteria that have been established to evaluate the options while looking for any biases that may be affecting the decision-making process.

This step is different from reviewing and challenging assumptions, as it focuses specifically on individual biases that may be affecting the decision maker rather than on assumptions related to the criteria. The goal of this step is to reduce the influence of cognitive biases on the decision-making process and ensure that the options are evaluated objectively and accurately.

Common cognitive biases that may influence decision-making include confirmation bias, anchoring bias, and sunk cost bias, among others. By recognizing these biases and considering counterevidence, decision-makers can reduce their influence and make more accurate and objective evaluations.

In summary, reviewing and challenging cognitive biases is an important step in the multi-criteria decision-making process that can help to ensure that the options are evaluated objectively and accurately. Whether this step should be combined with reviewing and challenging assumptions depends on the specific situation and the decision maker's preferences.

Key Question
Which cognitive biases might be affecting our decision-making process, and how can we reduce their influence for a more objective evaluation?

Process to Uncover Cognitive Biases
Here is a 10-step process in priority order one can use to root out cognitive biases in a multi-criteria decision-making process.

1. Identify Potential Biases
Start by identifying the potential cognitive biases that may be affecting your decision-making process. Common biases

include confirmation bias, anchoring bias, and sunk cost bias, among others.

2. Gather Information

Collect information and data that can help you validate or invalidate the biases. This may involve conducting research, consulting with experts, or gathering feedback from stakeholders.

3. Seek out Alternative Perspectives

Seek opinions and perspectives from people with different experiences, backgrounds, or expertise. This can help to challenge and broaden your thinking and reduce the influence of biases. Seek input from others, especially those with different viewpoints, to reveal any hidden biases.

4. Engage Stakeholders

Involve individuals with vested interests in the decision to ensure you have a variety of perspectives to consider and more thoughtful deliberation.

5. Consider Counterevidence.

Consider the evidence that contradicts the biases and weigh it against the evidence that supports the biases.

6. Get Feedback from Others.

Seek feedback from others, such as colleagues or experts, on the criteria that have been established. This can help to uncover any biases that may be affecting the decision-making process.

7. Consider Multiple Sources of Information

Consider multiple sources of information, such as data, research, or expert opinions, to validate the criteria. This can help to reduce the influence of cognitive biases.

8. Use Objective Measures.

Use objective measures, such as data and statistics, to evaluate the options and reduce the influence of biases.

9. Consider Multiple Options

Consider multiple options and evaluate each option based on the criteria. This can help to reduce the influence of biases and ensure that all options are evaluated objectively.

10. Re-evaluate and Adjust the Criteria

Continuously re-evaluate and adjust the criteria as new information becomes available. This can help to reduce the influence of cognitive biases and ensure that the criteria are up-to-date and relevant.

By following this process, you can root out cognitive biases and ensure that the criteria used to evaluate options in a multi-criteria decision-making process are objective. It's essential to be aware of your own biases and to be open-minded and willing to change your thinking as new information becomes available. By doing so, you can make more accurate and objective evaluations.

Examples of Cognitive Bias

Here are a few examples of how cognitive biases can impact the criteria for the house decision-making example:

Confirmation Bias. A decision maker may have a preconceived idea about the type of house they want and may only consider criteria that support this preconceived notion. For example, if the decision maker has a strong preference for a certain neighborhood, they may overlook other important criteria such as the condition of the house or the quality of the schools.

Anchoring Bias. The decision maker may be influenced by an initial impression of the house, such as the first price they see, and may ignore other important criteria. For example, if the first house they see is overpriced, they may assume that all other houses in the area are similarly priced and ignore other factors such as the quality of the neighborhood or the condition of the house.

Sunk Cost Bias. The decision maker may be influenced by the time and effort they have already invested in the decision-making process and may overlook other important criteria. For example, if they have already spent a significant amount of time searching for a house in a particular area, they may be less likely to consider houses in other areas, even if they would be a better fit based on other criteria.

Availability Bias. The decision maker may be influenced by information that is readily available or easily accessible and may ignore other important criteria. For example, if they rely solely on online listings or real estate agents for information about houses, they may overlook important criteria such as the quality of the neighborhood or the condition of the house.

These examples illustrate how cognitive biases can impact the criteria used in the decision-making process and lead to suboptimal decisions. By recognizing these biases and considering counterevidence, decision-makers can reduce their influence and make more accurate and objective evaluations.

6. Develop a Rubric for Each Criterion to Score the Options

Designing an effective scoring rubric for each criterion is foundational in evaluating and comparing options.

Creating a rubric for each criterion to score the options is a crucial step in the multi-criteria decision-making process. A rubric provides a clear and consistent method for objectively evaluating the options based on each criterion and allows for more effective comparison and ranking of the options.

There are two main types of scoring systems for a rubric: quantitative and qualitative. While qualitative scoring systems use subjective descriptions, such as "excellent" or "poor," quantitative scoring systems use numerical values, such as a 1-10 scale.

Quantitative scoring systems are preferred in decision-making because they provide a more objective and accurate evaluation of the options. Numerical values are easier to compare and interpret, and they provide a more precise method for ranking the options. Additionally, quantitative scoring systems allow for more nuanced evaluations, as they allow decision-makers to consider multiple factors when scoring the options.

When creating a rubric, it is important to clearly define each criterion and establish a numerical scoring system. The scores should be clear and consistent and should take into account the relative importance of each criterion. The rubric should be regularly reviewed and updated to ensure it remains relevant and accurate as new information becomes available.

Key Question
What is an effective scoring rubric for each criterion, and how can it be designed to ensure a consistent and objective evaluation of options in the multi-criteria decision-making process?

Designing a Rubric Scoring Process

1. **Define the Criteria.** Clearly define each criterion and ensure that it is specific and measurable.
2. **Establish a Quantitative Scoring System:** Establish a numerical scoring system, such as a 1-10 scale, to evaluate the options based on each criterion.
3. **Define the Scores.** Define the numerical scores for each criterion and ensure they are clear and consistent.
4. **Consider Multiple Factors.** Consider multiple factors, such as the relative importance of each criterion, when defining the scores.
5. **Regularly review and update.** Regularly review and update the rubric to ensure it remains relevant and accurate.

Creating a quantitative rubric for each criterion to score the options is an essential step in the multi-criteria decision-making process. Quantitative scoring systems provide a more objective and accurate evaluation of the options and allow for a clear and consistent method of comparison and ranking. By following best practices, decision-makers can create a robust and effective rubric to help them achieve their goals.

Using the example of purchasing a home in a suburban neighborhood, these are potential scoring rubric for each of the ten criteria based on the process noted above:

1. Price

0: The home is significantly over budget

2-4: The home is slightly over budget

4-6: The home is within budget

7-9: The home is below budget

10: The home is significantly below budget

2. Location

0: The home is located in an undesirable neighborhood

2-4: The home is located in a less-desirable neighborhood

4-6: The home is located in a desirable neighborhood

7-9: The home is located in a highly desirable neighborhood

10: The home is located in an exceptional neighborhood

3. Size

0: The home is significantly too small to accommodate family needs

2-4: The home is slightly too small to accommodate your family's needs

4-6: The home has enough bedrooms and space to accommodate family

7-9: The home has extra bedrooms and space to allow for expansion

10: The home has significantly more bedrooms and living space

4. Layout

0: The floor plan is not suitable for your lifestyle and preferences

2-4: The floor plan has some flaws that make it less suitable for your

4-6: The floor plan is suitable for your lifestyle and preferences

7-9: The floor plan has features that make it more suitable for lifestyle

10: The floor plan is exceptional and meets all lifestyle preferences

5. Nice Kitchen

0: The kitchen is outdated and not functional or attractive

2-4: The kitchen is outdated but has some attractive elements

4-6: The kitchen is functional and has some attractive elements

7-9: The kitchen is both functional and highly attractive

10: The kitchen is exceptional and has all the desired features

6. Big Backyard

0: The backyard is small and not suitable for outdoor activities

2-4: The backyard is small but has some potential for outdoor activities

4-6: The backyard is a suitable size for outdoor activities

7-9: The backyard is large and has good potential for outdoor activities

10: The backyard is exceptional and ideal for outdoor activities

7. School District

0: The local schools are below average and have major concerns

2-4: The local schools are below average and have some concerns

4-6: The local schools are average and have some concerns

7-9: The local schools are above average and have some strengths

10: The local schools are exceptional and have many strengths

8. Safety and Crime Rate

0: The neighborhood is unsafe, with high crime rates

2-4: The neighborhood is somewhat unsafe, with moderate crime rates

4-6: The neighborhood is safe, with low crime rates

7-9: The neighborhood is highly safe, with very low crime rates

10: The neighborhood is exceptionally safe, with almost no crime rates

9. Property Condition

0: The home is in poor condition and requires significant repairs

2-4: The home is in fair condition and requires some repairs or upgrades

4-6: The home is in good condition but may require some minor repairs

7-9: The home is in excellent condition and requires only minimal repairs

10: The home is in pristine condition and does not require any repairs

10. Potential for Appreciation

0: The home has poor potential for increasing in value over time

2-4: The home has some potential for increasing in value over time

4-6: The home has good potential for increasing in value over time

7-9: The home has excellent potential for increasing in value over time

10: The home has exceptional potential for increasing in value over time

A scoring rubric provides a *clear* and **consistent** method for evaluating each of the ten criteria in the multi-criteria decision-making process. By using a numerical scoring system, decision-makers can make more objective and accurate evaluations and comparisons of the options. Regularly reviewing and updating the rubric will ensure it remains relevant and accurate.

7.   Prioritize and Weigh Criteria

Prioritizing and Assigning Weights to Criteria for Informed Decision-making

Effectively prioritizing and assigning weight to each criterion is the crucial next step in the decision-making process. This helps to ensure that your decision is based on a balanced consideration of all relevant factors. This step is often left out, and this "neglect" is a critical mistake in any decision process. It is common sense that not all criteria should have the same impact on a decision.

Key Question

How can we accurately prioritize and weigh the criteria to ensure a balanced and well-informed decision?

---

3 Methods for Prioritizing Criteria and Assigning Weights

There are three methods for prioritizing a list of criteria and assigning weights to each criterion: the List Comparison Method, the Pairwise Comparison Method, and the Analytic Hierarchy Process (AHP).

1.   List Comparison Method

The List Comparison Method focuses on prioritizing a list of criteria by comparing each criterion with subsequent items in the list iteratively. It breaks down the process into smaller, manageable comparisons to minimize cognitive overload and reduce the likelihood of errors. This method is ideal for situations where the main goal is to create a prioritized list without necessarily quantifying the relative importance of each criterion. The strengths of this method include simplicity and ease of use, while its weaknesses include potential subjectivity and lack of a quantitative process to calculate each criterion's relative importance (the weight).

2. Pairwise Comparison Method

The Pairwise Comparison Method prioritizes a list of criteria and assigns weights to each criterion through pairwise comparisons. It involves comparing each criterion with every other criterion in terms of their relative importance or preference. This method provides a more structured approach to decision-making by assigning weights to each criterion based on their relative importance. The strengths of this method include its ability to quantify the relative importance of each criterion and its comprehensive approach, while its weaknesses include its complexity compared to the List Comparison Method.

3. Analytic Hierarchy Process (AHP)[30]

The AHP is an advanced version of the Pairwise Comparison Method. It not only prioritizes criteria and assigns weights to each criterion but also assesses the consistency of the decision maker's judgments. This method is most suitable for situations where decision makers need to transparently and quantitatively evaluate multiple criteria and their relative importance. The strengths of AHP include its ability to quantify the relative importance of each criterion, its comprehensive approach, and the inclusion of consistency checking, while its weaknesses include its complexity and the need for a more in-depth understanding of the pairwise comparison process.

---

[30] Saaty, T. L. (1980). The Analytic Hierarchy Process: Planning, Priority Setting, Resource Allocation. New York: McGraw-Hill.

To summarize, the List Comparison Method is more straightforward and suitable for creating a prioritized list without necessarily quantifying the relative importance of each criterion. On the other hand, the Pairwise Comparison Method and the Analytic Hierarchy Process provide more structured and quantifiable approaches to decision-making by prioritizing criteria and assigning weights to each criterion. The choice between these methods depends on the specific requirements of the decision-making process and the level of detail and quantification needed.

The 3 Methods in Practice
See the Appendix for how the three methods of prioritizing criteria are used in practice.

1. List Comparison Method
The List Comparison Method is a two-part process. First, put the criteria into *priority order*. Second, *assign weights* to each criterion. We will describe these two steps below.

Part 1: Prioritizing the Criteria
Putting the list of criteria into prioritized order is a two-step process:

> **Step 1: List Comparison.** Begin by comparing the first item in your list of criteria with each subsequent item. Whenever you find an item that is a higher priority than the current first item, replace the first item with the higher priority item. Move the previous first item to second place on the list. Now compare the "new" first item against each of the other items in the list. Continue this process until you reach the end of the list. Once you reach the end of the list, this means that you have compared it to all other items, and this item can now be *locked into the first position*. It no longer needs to be compared to any other items on the list. It is locked into its priority order location on the list.

Step 2: Iterative Process. Continue the list comparison process for the remaining items, starting with the second item in the list and locking each subsequent highest priority item into its respective position once you have reached the end of the list for that item. Repeat the process until all criteria are ranked in priority order.

The List Comparison Method effectively prioritizes a list by breaking the process down into smaller, manageable comparisons, avoiding the overwhelming nature of multitasking and reducing the likelihood of errors. Focusing on one comparison at a time allows for a more accurate assessment of each criterion's relative importance and minimizes cognitive overload. This methodical approach also minimizes the impact of subjective biases, ensuring that decisions align with priorities and objectives. In summary, the list comparison method simplifies the prioritization process, enabling a more systematic and accurate evaluation of criteria, ultimately leading to better decision making.

Part 2: Weighing the Criteria

The List Comparison Method doesn't provide a mathematical formula to assign weights to the criteria. It mainly focuses on prioritizing the criteria in a list. However, you can use the resulting prioritized list to assign weights based on their order and using "best judgement". Alternatively, you can also use a mathematical scale. There are two different types of scales.

Linear Scale

One way to assign weights is by using a simple linear scale. For example, if you have 10 criteria, you can assign the highest priority criterion a weight of 10, the second highest a weight of 9, and so on until the lowest priority criterion has a weight of 1. This way, the weights reflect the prioritized order of the criteria.

Exponential and Logarithmic Scales

Alternatively, you can use a different scale to emphasize the importance of the highest priority criteria, such as *exponential* or *logarithmic* scales. This would involve assigning higher weights to the top criteria and lower weights to the less important ones, with the difference in weights increasing as the criteria become more important. Exponential and logarithmic scales are related but not the same. They are, in fact, inverse functions of each other. However, when it comes to prioritizing criteria and assigning weights in decision-making processes, both exponential and logarithmic scales can be used to emphasize the importance of higher priority criteria.

An *exponential scale* uses a base raised to the power of the rank (or some other transformation) to assign weights. Higher priority criteria receive exponentially greater weights than lower priority criteria. As you move down the priority list, the weights decrease rapidly.

On the other hand, a *logarithmic scale* assigns weights based on the logarithm of the rank (or some other transformation) to the base. With a logarithmic scale, the difference between weights becomes smaller as you move down the priority list, making the lower priority criteria relatively more important than in an exponential scale.

Both exponential and logarithmic scales can be adjusted by changing the base, which affects the rate at which the weights decrease. The choice between these scales (or a linear scale) will depend on the specific decision-making context and the desired emphasis on higher-priority criteria compared to lower-priority criteria. The choice of scale depends on how critical the differences in priority are for your specific decision-making context.

2.   Pairwise Comparison Method

The Pairwise Comparison Method involves three main steps to prioritize *and* assign weights to criteria in decision-making. First, each pair of criteria is compared to determine their relative importance using a simple scale. Next, the weight of each criterion is calculated based on the assigned values during the comparisons, resulting in a percentage weight. Lastly, the weights are normalized. Note that this method prioritizes and weighs the criteria in the same step.

- **Pairwise Comparison.** For each pair of criteria, determine which criterion is more important to the decision and to what extent. You can use a simple scale (e.g., 1-5, with 1 being "equally important" and 5 being "significantly more important") to quantify the relative importance of each criterion.
- **Weight Calculation.** Calculate the weight of each criterion by summing the values assigned to it during the pairwise comparisons and then dividing by the total sum of values for all criteria. This will give you a percentage weight for each criterion.
- **Normalize Weights.** Ensure that the sum of all percentage weights equals 100%. If necessary, adjust the weights slightly so that they add up to 100%, while maintaining their relative importance.

3. Analytic Hierarchy Process (AHP)

AHP is a more advanced method for prioritizing and assigning weights to criteria, encompassing three main steps. First, criteria are compared pairwise to determine their relative importance using a predefined scale, and a comparison matrix is formed. Next, the eigenvector method is applied to calculate the weights of each criterion, providing a more accurate representation of their importance. Finally, the consistency ratio is calculated to validate the coherence of the decision maker's judgments, ensuring the reliability of the derived priority rankings and weights.

AHP is most suitable in decision-making situations where there are multiple criteria that need to be considered and there are trade-offs between these criteria. AHP is particularly useful when:

There are Multiple Criteria. AHP is designed to handle decision-making situations where there are multiple criteria that need to be considered. It allows decision-makers to systematically and consistently compare alternatives based on these criteria.

Criteria have Different Weights. AHP allows decision-makers to assign weights to each criterion based on its relative importance. This helps to ensure that the decision is made based on the most important criteria.

Criteria are Interdependent. AHP recognizes that criteria are often interdependent and that changes in one criterion may affect the evaluation of others. It allows decision-makers to capture these interdependencies and make more informed decisions.

Subjectivity is Involved. AHP can accommodate subjective judgments and preferences of decision-makers through the use of pairwise comparisons. This allows decision makers to incorporate their expertise and knowledge into the decision-making process.

Some examples of decision-making situations where AHP may be most suitable include resource allocation, project selection, supplier selection, product design, and investment decision-making.

Overall, AHP is a powerful tool for decision-making in complex situations where multiple criteria need to be considered, and trade-offs need to be made between these criteria.

Although AHP can be a useful tool in many decision-making situations, there are some cases where it may not be suitable. For example, AHP may not be suitable in the following situations:

When There are Only a Few Criteria. If there are only a few criteria to consider, AHP may not be necessary, and a simpler decision-making tool may be more appropriate.

When There is no Clear Hierarchy. AHP assumes that the criteria can be arranged in a hierarchy, with the higher-level criteria representing more abstract and general factors and the lower-level criteria representing more specific and concrete factors. If there is no clear hierarchy among the criteria, AHP may not be suitable.

When There are Too Many Alternatives. AHP can become unwieldy when there are too many alternatives to evaluate. In such cases, a more efficient decision-making tool may be more appropriate.

When There is no Consensus. AHP relies on the consensus of decision-makers to generate meaningful results. If there is no consensus among the decision-makers, AHP may not be suitable.

When There is Insufficient Data. AHP requires data on the criteria and alternatives to be evaluated. If there is insufficient data, AHP may not be suitable, and other decision-making tools may be more appropriate.

Overall, AHP is most suitable in decision-making situations where there are multiple criteria, trade-offs need to be made, and there is a clear hierarchy among the criteria. However, decision-makers should carefully consider the appropriateness of AHP for their specific decision-making situation and explore other decision-making tools if necessary.

    1. Pairwise Comparison. Compare each pair of criteria using a predefined scale (e.g., 1-9, with 1 indicating "equally important" and 9 signifying "extremely more important") to quantify their relative importance. Next, assign the inverse of the scale value for the opposite comparison (e.g., if A compared to B is 3, then B compared to A is 1/3).

2. Comparison Matrix. Create a matrix by inputting the pairwise comparison values. For each criterion, divide the comparison value by the sum of the values in their respective column. Calculate the average of the normalized values in each row to obtain the priority vector, which represents the weights of the criteria.

3. Eigenvector Calculation. Multiply the comparison matrix by the priority vector to obtain the eigenvector. Then, divide each element in the eigenvector by the corresponding element in the priority vector to obtain the eigenvalue. Calculate the average eigenvalue (λ_max).

4. Consistency Index and Ratio. Determine the consistency index (CI) by subtracting the number of criteria (n) from the average eigenvalue (λ_max) and dividing the result by (n-1). Compare the CI to the corresponding random index (RI) value, which is based on the number of criteria being compared. Calculate the consistency ratio (CR) by dividing the CI by the RI. A CR of 0.1 or lower indicates an acceptable level of consistency in the decision-maker's judgments.

8. Generate Options

To make a well-informed decision, it is essential to generate a diverse set of options that can be evaluated against your established criteria. Usually, people already have some options, and that's why they seek out a process to make the decision. But often, they don't realize they have other options. This step enables you to explore a wide range of possibilities and encourages creativity in the decision-making process. A comprehensive list of options increases the likelihood of finding an optimal solution that aligns with your objective and purpose.

Key Question
What is the process for generating a comprehensive
and diverse set of options to consider when making
a decision?

Process to Generate Options

This is a 4-step process that can be used to generate a diverse set of options that meet our criteria. Underneath each step is an example from our house-purchasing decision exercise.

1. **Brainstorming:** Gather a group of individuals with diverse perspectives and expertise to brainstorm potential options. Encourage open discussion and the sharing of ideas without judgment. This can lead to a richer set of options, as well as identifying previously unconsidered possibilities.

   For example, gather friends, family, or colleagues with diverse perspectives and experiences in real estate and home buying to brainstorm potential options. Encourage open discussion about different types of properties, locations, and financing options without judgment. This can lead to a richer set of housing options.

2. **Research:** Conduct thorough research to gather information on potential options, both within and outside your industry or area of expertise. Investigate best practices, innovative solutions, and lessons learned from similar situations or decisions.

   For example, research potential neighborhoods, property types, and market trends. Investigate best practices for home buying, innovative solutions for financing or negotiation, and lessons learned from others who have recently purchased homes. Gather

information from various sources, such as real estate websites, government reports, and local forums.

3. **Consultation:** Seek input from experts, mentors, or colleagues who have experience in the area of your decision. Their insights and experiences can help you identify potential options or refine your existing options.

   For example, seek input from real estate agents, mortgage brokers, or financial advisors who have experience in the area of home buying. Their insights and experiences can help you identify potential housing options, provide guidance on the current market, and refine your existing options based on their expertise.

4. **Scenario Planning:** Develop multiple scenarios based on different assumptions or future conditions to explore a range of potential options. This approach helps you to anticipate various outcomes and identify options that are robust and adaptable to change.

   For example, consider how your housing options would fare in a market downturn or if your financial situation were to change.

   By following this 4-step process, you can generate a diverse set of housing options that meet your criteria, increasing your chances of finding the perfect home that aligns with your objectives and preferences.

9. Evaluate Individual Options: Pros and Cons

We're getting closer! This step weighs the merits and drawbacks of each option to determine which aligns best with your criteria and objectives. By systematically identifying the pros and cons and then attempting to mitigate the cons, you'll be well-equipped to decide how to score the options.

Key Question
How does each option perform against the
established criteria, and which option best aligns
with our objectives and purpose, considering the
pros, cons, and mitigated cons?

3 Step Process to Evaluate and Score

1. Identify the Pros and Cons of each Option

In this step, dedicate time to thoroughly analyze each option based on the established criteria. With a comprehensive understanding of each option's advantages and disadvantages, you can make better-informed choices. Encourage open discussion and collaboration with your team or decision-making group, as diverse perspectives can reveal aspects that may otherwise be overlooked. By identifying the pros and cons for each criterion, you ensure that every aspect of the decision is taken into account.

Note that this is where a SWOT Analysis (Strengths, Weaknesses, Opportunities, and Threats) can also be considered for each potential housing option. This will help you identify the strengths and weaknesses of each option, such as the location, price, size, and condition of the property. Additionally, it can uncover new possibilities, such as a renovation or investment opportunities, as well as potential risks, like required maintenance or neighborhood safety concerns.

For each house option, carefully analyze its pros and cons based on the established criteria such as location, price, size, condition, and neighborhood. For example, House A might have a great location and neighborhood but is slightly over budget and may need some renovations. Encourage open discussions with family members or other stakeholders to ensure everyone's perspectives are considered when identifying the pros and cons.

2. Mitigate Cons

After identifying the cons for each option, focus on finding ways to address, minimize, or even turn them into pros. This process requires a problem-solving mindset and a willingness to think outside the box. Engage in brainstorming sessions with your team or decision-making group to explore potential solutions or workarounds for the cons. By actively mitigating drawbacks, you can improve the overall quality of your options and enhance your decision-making process.

For example, if House A is over budget, consider negotiating the price with the seller, exploring financing options, or identifying cost-saving measures for the necessary renovations. Brainstorm with family members or your real estate agent to find creative solutions that can improve the overall attractiveness of each option.

This step proved to be a game-changer when I bought my first home. Having a spacious backyard was a top priority for me. I came across what seemed like my dream house – it met all my requirements, from budget and location to amenities. However, there was one significant drawback: the backyard was sloped and smaller than I had hoped. As someone who loves spending time outdoors, this felt like a deal-breaker.

But then, I decided to take a closer look using Google Maps. When I viewed the satellite image of the house, I discovered that it was adjacent to a 1,000-acre park, complete with bike trails and carriage trails. This park was connected to several other fantastic parks, together spanning thousands of acres. Suddenly, I realized that I had access to an even more incredible backyard than I had initially imagined.

With this revelation, my perspective changed entirely. The house and its unique backyard not only met my needs but exceeded my expectations, and I enjoyed many years of happiness there. This experience demonstrates the importance of thoroughly evaluating the cons and seeing if you can mitigate them in some fashion by considering alternative perspectives when making a decision.

3. Score Options

Once you have identified the pros and cons and mitigated the cons for each option, it's time to score them based on the rubric developed earlier in the process. The scoring process involves assigning a numerical value to each option for every criterion, considering the weights assigned to the criteria. This quantitative approach allows for objective comparison and ranking of the options, making it easier to identify the option that best aligns with your objectives and purpose. In addition, by scoring each option systematically, you can ensure that your final decision is both data-driven and well-informed.

For example, assign scores for each criterion like location, price, size, condition, and neighborhood, considering the weights assigned to each criterion. This scoring process will allow you to objectively compare and rank the house options, making it easier to determine which option best aligns with your objectives and purpose.

More specifically, refer back to the hypothetical rubric that we identified previously in our example and score House Option A:

1. Price Score: 3

   Rubric: 2-4: The home is slightly over budget

2. Location Score: 8

   Rubric: 7-9: The home is located in a highly desirable neighborhood

3. Size Score: 5

   Rubric: 4-6: The home has enough bedrooms and living space

4. Layout Score: 10

Rubric: 10: The floor plan is exceptional for lifestyle preferences

5. Kitchen Score: 8

Rubric: 7-9: The kitchen is both functional and highly attractive

6. Backyard Size: 0

Rubric: 0: The backyard is small and not suitable for activities

7. School District Score: 10

Rubric:10: The local schools are exceptional

8. Safety Score: 5

Rubric:4-6: The neighborhood is safe with low crime rates

9. Property Condition Score: 8

Rubric:7-9: The home is in excellent condition and requires minimal repairs

10. Potential for Appreciation Score: 8

Rubric:7-9: The home has excellent potential for increasing in value over time

As we can see, this house likely will score well except for the small backyard. However, when examining low scores, the mitigation of cons step may increase this score significantly depending on the mitigation and may in fact, even turn this low score into a high score, as it did for me when I discovered the adjoining parks. These scores will then be used in our next step.

10. Weigh Scoring Analysis: Integrate Criteria Importance into the Evaluation

---

Key Question
How do the weighted scores of each option
compare, and which option emerges as the most
suitable choice based on the combined weighted
scores?

Instructions for Performing Weighted Scoring Analysis

1. Retrieve the weights assigned to each criterion from the earlier steps in the decision-making process.
2. Multiply the score for each criterion by its corresponding weight for each option. This will give you the weighted score for that specific criterion and option.
3. Sum up the weighted scores for all criteria for each option. This will result in a total weighted score for each option.
4. Compare the total weighted scores of all options to determine which one has the highest score. This option is likely the best fit based on your established criteria and the importance you've assigned to each criterion.

In this example, we'll evaluate Option A, a potential home for purchase, using the weighted criteria scores from Step 7 and the individual scores from Step 9.

Step 7 - Prioritizing and Weighting Criteria (using the Linear Method of Weighting):

1. Affordability: 0.1818 (18.18%)
2. School district quality: 0.1636 (16.36%)
3. Neighborhood safety: 0.1455 (14.55%)

4. Commute time: 0.1273 (12.73%)
5. Proximity to amenities: 0.1091 (10.91%)
6. Number of bedrooms: 0.0909 (9.09%)
7. Number of bathrooms: 0.0727 (7.27%)
8. Nice kitchen: 0.0545 (5.45%)
9. Large backyard: 0.0364 (3.64%)
10. Home's overall condition: 0.0182 (1.82%)

Step 9 - Individual Scores for Option A:

1. Price: 3 (Slightly over budget)
2. Location: 8 (Highly desirable neighborhood)
3. Size: 5 (Adequate bedrooms and living space)
4. Layout: 10 (Exceptional floor plan)
5. Kitchen: 8 (Functional and highly attractive)
6. Backyard: 0 (Small and unsuitable for outdoor activities)
7. School District: 10 (Exceptional local schools)
8. Safety: 5 (Safe neighborhood with low crime rates)
9. Property Condition: 8 (Excellent condition, minimal repairs)
10. Appreciation Potential: 8 (High potential for value increase)

Calculating the Weighted Scores for Option A:

1. Price: $3 * 0.1818 = 0.5454$
2. Location: $8 * 0.1636 = 1.3088$
3. Size: $5 * 0.1455 = 0.7275$
4. Layout: $10 * 0.1273 = 1.2730$
5. Kitchen: $8 * 0.1091 = 0.8728$
6. Backyard: $0 * 0.0364 = 0.0000$
7. School District: $10 * 0.1636 = 1.6360$
8. Safety: $5 * 0.1455 = 0.7275$
9. Property Condition: $8 * 0.0182 = 0.1456$
10. Appreciation Potential: $8 * 0.0545 = 0.4360$

Summing the weighted scores for Option A: 0.5454 + 1.3088 + 0.7275 + 1.2730 + 0.8728 + 0.0000 + 1.6360 + 0.7275 + 0.1456 + 0.4360 = 7.6726

The final weighted score for Option A is 7.6726. After evaluating other options similarly, you can compare their weighted scores to identify the best choice based on your criteria and preferences.

Let's assume the weighted scores for Houses A through J are as follows:

1. House A: 7.6726
2. House B: 8.2345
3. House C: 7.1590
4. House D: 8.6789
5. House E: 7.9450
6. House F: 7.3925
7. House G: 8.1085
8. House H: 7.5130
9. House I: 7.8605
10. House J: 8.3900

Step 4 - Compare the total weighted scores of all options:

1. House D: 8.6789
2. House J: 8.3900
3. House B: 8.2345
4. House G: 8.1085
5. House E: 7.9450
6. House I: 7.8605
7. House A: 7.6726
8. House H: 7.5130
9. House F: 7.3925
10. House C: 7.1590

Based on the total weighted scores, House D is the "winner" based on our process so far, scoring the highest at 8.6789. This house aligns best with the established criteria and the importance assigned to each criterion. But is it really the winner? Read on...

Conclusion

Effective decision-making requires a structured and systematic approach, particularly for strategic decisions. This chapter has covered various processes and methods to improve decision-making, including a 10-step process for uncovering cognitive biases, developing a quantitative rubric for multi-criteria decision-making, and generating a diverse set of options to evaluate against established criteria. By following these best practices, decision-makers can ensure that their choices are aligned with their values and priorities, leading to better outcomes and greater success. Additionally, regularly reviewing and updating the decision-making process can help decision-makers adapt to changing circumstances and improve their decision-making skills over time. Whether you are a business leader, a team manager, or an individual making personal decisions, the information presented in this chapter can help you make well-informed and impactful decisions that contribute to lasting success.

Summary

1. Making decisions can be a complex and difficult process, particularly when dealing with complex issues.
2. Adopting a systematic strategy can help to improve the effectiveness of decision-making.
3. A structured approach involves breaking down the decision-making process into smaller steps.
4. Each step should be carefully considered and based on reliable information and data.
5. The process should involve input from stakeholders and experts.
6. A decision-making framework can be helpful in guiding the process.
7. An effective strategy should take into account potential risks and uncertainties.
8. Regular evaluation and monitoring of decisions can help to identify any issues or problems.
9. Effective communication is key to ensuring that all stakeholders are informed and on board with the decision.
10. Adopting a systematic strategy can help to ensure that decisions are made in a timely and efficient manner.

Questions

1. What is the benefit of adopting a systematic strategy for decision-making?

   It can improve the effectiveness of decision-making.

2. How should a decision-making process be structured?

   By breaking it down into smaller steps and considering them.

3. Why is it important to consider potential risks and uncertainties in the decision-making process?

   It ensures that any potential negative outcomes are identified.

4. What is the role of stakeholders in the process?

   To provide input and their perspectives.

5. What is the benefit of regular evaluation and monitoring of decisions?

   This can help to identify any issues or problems that may arise.

6. How can effective communication help to ensure effective decision-making?

   It can ensure that all stakeholders are informed of the decision.

7. How can a decision-making framework be helpful in the decision-making process?

   It provides structure to the decision-making process.

8. Why is it important to base decisions on reliable information?

   It can help to ensure that the decision is based on accurate and relevant information.

9. How can a systematic strategy help to ensure decisions are made in a timely manner?

   By breaking down the decision-making process into smaller steps.

10. What is the benefit of involving experts in the process?

    This can provide valuable insights and perspectives.

Exercises

1. Identify a decision you need to make in your personal or professional life. Then, create a decision-making framework with specific steps to guide the process.

2. Choose a complex issue you are currently facing. Then, break down the decision-making process into smaller steps and consider how each step can be informed by reliable information and data. Involve stakeholders and experts as needed.

3. Reflect on a past decision that did not turn out as planned. Analyze the decision-making process you used and identify areas where adopting a systematic strategy could have improved the outcome. Use this analysis to develop a framework for future decisions.

4. Conduct research on a proven decision-making strategy, such as the Six Thinking Hats method or the SWOT analysis. Apply this strategy to a decision and evaluate its effectiveness.

5. Take a decision-making training course or workshop to learn new systematic strategies for effective decision-making. Apply these strategies to a real-life decision and evaluate the outcome.

6. Pinpoint a decision you have been putting off. Then, develop a step-by-step plan for making the decision, including a timeline for completing each step. Follow this plan to make the decision and evaluate its effectiveness.

7. Practice gathering and analyzing data to inform your decision-making. Choose a topic of interest and collect data from a variety of sources. Use this data to make a decision.

8. Develop a risk management plan for a decision you need to make. Consider potential risks, and identify steps you can take to minimize or address them. Use this plan to guide your decision-making and evaluate its effectiveness.

9. Conduct a decision-making simulation with a group of colleagues or friends. Choose a complex issue and work through the decision-making process together using a structured approach.

10. Think about your decision-making style and preferences. Identify any biases or blind spots that may be affecting your decision-making. Develop strategies for mitigating these biases and apply them to a real-life decision.

Principle 7

Refine the Shortlist with Comparative Ranking

"You have to learn how to see the essence of each subject and then to learn how to make comparisons, to see what is similar and what is different." - Edward de Bono

Find the Winning Choice Through Strategic Comparisons

Refining the shortlist involves using comparative ranking to evaluate and prioritize options based on various factors, such as feasibility, potential outcomes, and costs. This allows you to make well-informed decisions because you are taking a structured and analytical approach. In addition, ranking the options on the shortlist allows for prioritization based on their strengths and weaknesses, resulting in better outcomes.

Key Question

How do our top contenders compare against each other in terms of the established criteria, and which option emerges as the most suitable choice when assessed through a head-to-head comparison?

This chapter delves into the crucial step of refining your top-scoring options through a comparative ranking process. This approach helps you to sharpen your focus and gain a deeper understanding of how the top contenders stack up against each other in terms of individual criteria. In addition, using a relative ranking method to re-evaluate your shortlist can help you make a more thorough, informed decision.

Comparative Scoring

Comparative scoring is a decision-making technique that involves comparing and ranking options directly against each other based on their relative performance in each criterion. This method differs from criteria-based scoring, which assigns a score to each option based on how well it meets each criterion. One of the reasons comparative scoring can be more effective than criteria-based scoring is that it narrows the focus on the most relevant and competitive options. By comparing options head-to-head, you can more easily identify the subtle differences that may not be as apparent when evaluating options independently. This process can lead to a more accurate assessment of the overall suitability of each option.

However, going through the criteria-based scoring process *first* to eliminate weaker candidates and create a shortlist of top contenders. This step ensures that the comparative scoring process remains manageable and efficient, as comparing many options can be time-consuming and challenging.

A study conducted by the National Bureau of Economic Research (NBER) found that using criteria-based scoring in hiring can lead to more diverse and qualified applicant pools. The study analyzed data from a large-scale field experiment in which employers were randomly assigned to use a traditional resume-based or a more structured, criteria-based screening process. The results showed that the criteria-based screening process led to a more diverse applicant pool and a higher proportion of highly qualified applicants compared to the resume-based screening process. Specifically, the study found that the criteria-based screening process led to a 23% increase in the proportion of highly qualified applicants and a 36% increase in the proportion of female applicants compared to the resume-based screening process.[31]

After completing this initial assessment, comparative scoring can be applied to fine-tune the decision and determine the best option among the shortlisted candidates.

1.   Shortlist the Top Contenders

To make the most effective use of comparative scoring, it is crucial to identify and narrow down the highest-scoring options from your initial analysis. Focusing on the top contenders ensures that your time and energy are directed toward evaluating the most promising options. Review the scores obtained through the criteria-based scoring process and select the options with the highest overall scores. This shortlist will serve as the basis for your comparative ranking process.

2.   Head-to-Head Comparison

Once you have shortlisted the top contenders, it is time to conduct a head-to-head comparison by evaluating them against each other based on each criterion. This process involves closely examining each option's relative strengths and weaknesses and noting any aspects that distinguish them from one another. By comparing the options directly, you gain a deeper understanding of their overall suitability and performance within your specific decision-making criteria.

3.   Quantify the Differences

In the comparative scoring process, it is essential to quantify the differences between the top contenders to assign new scores based on their relative performance. To ensure a more thorough evaluation of shortlist contenders, ask and account for a further

---

[31] Sackett, P. R., Lievens, F., & Van Iddekinge, C. H. (2021). Using situational judgment tests to increase diversity in applicant pools: Evidence from a large-scale field experiment. Journal of Applied Psychology, 106(1), 61–81. https://doi.org/10.1037/apl0000518

question beyond ranking the contenders: *Contender B is better than Contender C but by how much?*

Techniques such as pairwise comparison — comparing each option with every other option in terms of a specific criterion and assigning a score based on which option performs — or ranking can be used to determine the degree of difference between options for each criterion. By quantifying the differences, you create an even clearer picture of the options' performance and can more easily identify the most suitable choice.

4. Re-evaluate the Weighted Scores

After completing the comparative ranking process, it is necessary to update the weighted scores for your shortlisted options. Incorporate the new insights gained from the head-to-head comparison into the scoring process, adjusting the scores and weights as needed to reflect the relative performance of each option. This updated scoring will accurately represent each option's suitability, ensuring that your final decision is well-informed and based on the most relevant information.

Examples of Comparative Ranking

Let's assume we have already scored ten houses (A-J) based on the criteria and weighted scoring method discussed earlier. After reviewing the scores, we shortlist the top three contenders (Houses B, D, and F) for a more detailed comparative analysis.

Shortlisting Top Contenders – Rubric Scoring

House B: Weighted Score = 78

House D: Weighted Score = 76

House F: Weighted Score = 74

Head-to-Head Comparison

We now compare Houses B, D, and F against each other based on each criterion, focusing on their relative strengths and weaknesses.

Affordability: House D is the most affordable, followed by House B and F.

School district quality: House B is in the best school district, with House F slightly behind and House D in third place.

Large backyard: House F has the largest backyard, followed by House B, and House D has the smallest backyard.

Quantifying the Differences

We assign new scores based on the relative performance of each option in the head-to-head comparison using a 1-10 scale. For instance:

Affordability: House D (10 pts), House B (6 pts), House F (3 pts)

School district quality: House B (10 pts), House F (8 pts), House D (4 pts)

Large backyard: House F (10 pts), House B (7 pts), House D (2 pts)

Continue this process for all criteria.

Re-evaluating the Weighted Scores

Using the new scores from the head-to-head comparison, we update the weighted scores for the shortlisted options, incorporating the new insights gained.

House B: Updated Weighted Score = 82

House D: Updated Weighted Score = 78

House F: Updated Weighted Score = 80

B is still the winner, but notice that D and F switched spots. SoB is the winner! Or is it? Read on.

Conclusion

Refining your decision-making process through comparative ranking is crucial in choosing the most suitable option. Comparative scoring helps narrow down the most relevant and competitive options by comparing them head-to-head, enabling decision-makers to identify subtle differences that may not be apparent when evaluating options independently. It's essential to first go through the criteria-based scoring process to create a shortlist of top contenders. This shortlist provides the basis for the comparative ranking process, where decision-makers conduct a head-to-head comparison by evaluating the options against each other based on each criterion. Quantifying the differences between the top contenders is critical to assigning new scores based on their relative performance, resulting in an updated scoring system that accurately represents the option's suitability. The ultimate goal is to make a well-informed decision based on the most relevant information.

Summary

1. Refining your shortlist through a comparative ranking process can help you make a more informed and well-rounded decision.

2. Comparative scoring involves directly comparing and ranking options based on their relative performance in each criterion.

3. Shortlisting the highest-scoring options is necessary before conducting a head-to-head comparison.

4. Quantifying the differences between options can help assign new scores based on their relative performance.

5. Re-evaluating the weighted scores after the comparative ranking process can provide a more accurate representation of an option's suitability.

6. Comparative scoring allows for a more focused and in-depth evaluation of the top contenders, emphasizing their strengths and weaknesses relative to one another.

7. Comparative scoring can lead to a more accurate assessment of the overall suitability of each option.

8. Criteria-based scoring provides a solid foundation for the decision-making process by identifying the most promising options based on predefined criteria.

9. A head-to-head comparison involves evaluating the top contenders against each other based on each criterion.

10. Incorporating new insights gained from the head-to-head comparison can lead to a more informed and well-rounded final decision.

Questions

1. What is comparative scoring?

   A technique that directly compares and ranks options.

2. Why is it important to shortlist the highest-scoring options before conducting a head-to-head comparison?

   It directs you toward evaluating the best options.

3. How can quantifying the differences between options help in the comparative ranking process?

   It helps assign new scores based on their relative performance.

4. What are the benefits of re-evaluating the weighted scores?

   New insights are gained from head-to-head comparison.

5. What is the difference between criteria-based and comparative scoring?

   Criteria-based scoring scores each option, while comparative scoring compares and ranks options directly against each other.

6. How can comparative scoring lead to a more accurate assessment of each option?

   It allows for a more focused evaluation of the top contenders.

7. How does criteria-based scoring help with decision-making?

   It provides a solid foundation for the decision-making process.

8. What is the head-to-head comparison?

   Evaluating the top contenders against each other.

9. Why quantify differences between options?

   It creates an even clearer picture of the options' performance.

10. How does comparative ranking help identify the top contenders?

    By evaluating their relative performance in each criterion.

Exercises

1. Choose a real-life decision you need to make and identify the criteria that will be used to evaluate the options. Use criteria-based scoring to create a shortlist of top contenders. Then, conduct a head-to-head comparison of the shortlisted options using comparative scoring and re-evaluate the weighted scores based on the results.

2. Practice quantifying the differences between options using pairwise comparison or ranking. Choose a decision you must make and evaluate the top contenders using this technique.

3. Select a complex issue you currently face and break down the decision-making process into smaller steps. Identify the highest-scoring options and conduct a head-to-head comparison of the shortlisted options using comparative ranking.

4. Identify a past decision you made and evaluate it using comparative ranking. Determine whether applying this technique could have led to a more informed decision.

5. Develop a comparative ranking framework for a decision you need to make. Identify the criteria that will be used to evaluate the options.

6. Practice conducting a head-to-head comparison of options using real-life scenarios with a complex decision.

7. Research the different techniques for comparative ranking, such as pairwise comparison or ranking. Apply one of these techniques to a decision you need to make.

8. Reflect on a past decision you made that did not turn out as planned. Analyze the process you used and identify areas where applying comparative ranking can improve the outcome.

9. Hold a decision-making simulation with a group of colleagues or friends. Choose a complex issue and work through the decision-making process together, using comparative ranking to refine the shortlist of top contenders.

10. Identify a decision you must make and practice re-evaluating the weighted scores after the comparative ranking process. Incorporate the new insights gained from the head-to-head comparison into the scoring process, adjusting the scores and weights as needed to reflect the relative performance of each option.

Principle 8

Balance Logic and Intuition

"Intuition will tell the thinking mind where to look next."

- Jonas Salk

Use Instincts Through Intuitive Insights with Systematic Analysis

Balancing logic and intuition in decision-making is crucial for achieving a well-rounded, effective approach. Both analytical thinking and intuition have their strengths and limitations, and by recognizing and balancing them appropriately, you can make more comprehensive, nuanced decisions.

Key Question

How does our intuition align with the results of the comparative ranking process, and how can we use our gut feeling to inform and refine our final decision?

In this chapter, we explore the crucial role of intuition in the decision-making process. While the previous chapters have focused on objective criteria and systematic evaluations, it is essential to acknowledge that our "gut" feelings and instincts also play a significant role in helping us determine the best choice. By integrating intuition with logical analysis, you can arrive at a more comprehensive and confident decision that aligns with your rational goals and your emotional preferences.

What is Intuition?

Intuition is a form of knowing or understanding something without conscious reasoning or analytical thought. It is often described as a gut feeling, instinct, or an immediate sense of knowing that arises without any clear evidence or logical explanation. Intuition is thought to be a product of the subconscious mind, drawing on past experiences, patterns, and knowledge that may not be immediately accessible to our conscious awareness. Intuition is when you think you have the answer to a problem, and you say to yourself: "I can't quite put my finger on it. What am I missing?"

While intuition can sometimes lead to accurate insights and judgments, it can also be influenced by cognitive biases and emotional reactions, making it an imperfect guide for decision-making. As such, intuition often must be balanced with logic to arrive at the best decision.

A study published in the *Academy of Management Journal* found that intuitive decision-making can be effective in situations where the decision-maker has a high level of expertise in the relevant domain. Further, the study found that experts who used their intuition were more accurate in their decision-making than those who relied solely on analytical reasoning.[32]

At this stage in the decision-making process, you have diligently applied logic and analysis to evaluate and compare your options. While it is common to lean towards reason and objective criteria, it's essential not to dismiss the value of intuition entirely. Our instincts can provide valuable insights derived from our past experiences, emotions, and subconscious knowledge.

Jonas Salk's quotation emphasizes the complementary relationship between intuition and reason, suggesting that our gut feelings can guide our rational mind to explore areas that might have been overlooked or underappreciated during the analytical process. By conducting a gut check and examining

---

[32] Dane, E., & Pratt, M. G. (2007). Exploring intuition and its role in managerial decision making. Academy of Management Journal, 50(1), 1-13. https://doi.org/10.5465/amj.2007.24160888

your feelings toward the ranked options, you allow your intuition to highlight any discrepancies or areas that need further investigation.

If an option doesn't "feel" right, even though it ranks high based on the logical analysis, it's essential to dig deeper and identify the underlying reasons for the dissonance. For example, there may be hidden factors or personal values that haven't been explicitly considered in the criteria-based evaluation, which could significantly impact your decision.

Cognitive Dissonance

Recognizing the potential influence of cognitive dissonance on your decision-making process is essential. Cognitive dissonance refers to the mental discomfort or psychological stress that a person experiences when they hold two or more contradictory beliefs, values, or attitudes simultaneously. In the context of decision-making, cognitive dissonance could potentially emerge in the process when your logical analysis and intuition conflict with each other. For example, if your gut feeling tells you that a certain option is the best choice, but your objective analysis ranks it lower, you might experience cognitive dissonance.

> *In a classic study by Leon Festinger and colleagues, participants who were paid $1 to tell a lie about a boring task experienced more cognitive dissonance than those who were paid $20 to tell the same lie (Festinger & Carlsmith, 1959). This is because the $1 group had to justify why they lied to themselves, while the $20 group had an external justification for their behavior.*[33]

Addressing cognitive dissonance in your decision-making process can be beneficial. You can do this by re-examining your criteria, weighting, or assumptions or further exploring the reasons behind your intuitive feelings. This process can guide

---

[33] Festinger, L., & Carlsmith, J. M. (1959). Cognitive consequences of forced compliance. The Journal of Abnormal and Social Psychology, 58(2), 203-210.

you toward reconciling any conflicts between your logical analysis and your intuitive instincts.

When faced with a situation where your intuition or feeling about a decision doesn't reconcile with the score, it can indicate an error in the scoring model. This error could be due to improperly scored criteria or missing criteria altogether.

An example from my experience at Blue Ridge Capital demonstrates the importance of acknowledging and addressing cognitive dissonance in the decision-making process.

Intuition to the Rescue

At Blue Ridge Capital, my team and I needed to make an important decision with respect to scoring counterparty vendors for a critical function — Fund Administration. Having trained my team in the decision-making process described in this book (we used the decision matrix for all important decisions), I insisted on being involved only in weighing the criteria for scoring purposes. I considered this to be the most crucial part of the process. My team then diligently conducted their due diligence and scored each option. They proudly returned to me with the results and declared Citco as the winner. I had expected Morgan Stanley to win based on my intuition, but I was committed to making decisions based on logic, not emotion.

When they announced Citco as the winner, they could see my surprise. I asked them a few questions, and everything seemed right with the scoring, but I couldn't shake the uneasy feeling I had about the decision. They loved seeing me in this state of cognitive dissonance and proudly said, "You just wanted Morgan Stanley to win because you know everybody there!" A lightbulb went off in my head. I said, "You're right! I do!" Then I asked the key question: "Did we factor in the importance of the relationship as a criterion when scoring the vendors?" Sullen looks were exchanged all around the room, and my CFO told me sheepishly, "Um. No." I knew very few people at Citco.

I asked them to go back, give "relationship" a relatively heavy weighting, then come back to me after it was re-scored, and we would abide by the decision. Of course, after it was re-scored, Morgan Stanley won. The point here is not to manipulate the decision matrix to get the desired outcome but rather to listen to your intuition and use it to identify any inconsistencies or gaps in the decision-making process.

By recognizing and addressing the cognitive dissonance I experienced, we were able to make a more informed decision that ultimately proved to be the right choice. The relationship with Morgan Stanley has been crucial over the years, paying dividends and validating the importance of incorporating intuition into the decision-making process. In hindsight, Morgan Stanley was by far the correct decision, not because they were better or worse, but because, as I suspected in that moment of decision, I would be able to leverage my relationship with them over and over through the years — and that's exactly what I did. I believe this experience is what Jonas Salk had in mind when he said that "Intuition will tell the thinking mind where to look next."

Two "Famous People" Examples

Steve Jobs and the iPhone

Steve Jobs, the co-founder of Apple, relied heavily on his intuition when he envisioned the iPhone. He saw the potential of a touchscreen device that could replace multiple gadgets and transform the way people communicate. Jobs' intuitive decision to develop the iPhone revolutionized the smartphone industry and changed the way people interact with technology.

Warren Buffett and His Investments

Warren Buffett, one of the most successful investors in history, often credits his intuition for helping him make wise investment decisions. While he uses rigorous analysis and research to evaluate potential investments, he also trusts his gut when making crucial decisions.

Trust your Instincts?

Maybe. Intuition may serve as a valuable guide in the decision-making process but be cognizant that the experts have tested this out. The real benefits come when you have gained expertise and experience in a specific domain. Otherwise, your intuition may be clouded by the emotions and cognitive biases we discussed.

The Interplay Between Intuition and Logic: Two Scenarios

Emergency Decision-Making

In high-stress situations, such as medical emergencies or natural disasters, intuition can play a vital role in helping us make quick and effective decisions. However, these intuitive decisions are often backed by the expertise and knowledge gained through years of training and experience.

Emergency decision-making often demands swift action, which is where intuition can play a vital role. A personal experience demonstrates this point vividly.

> *When faced with an emergency flood leak alarm in my home, I rushed to the basement to investigate the source of the problem. Upon jumping up to inspect the water closet, I accidentally impaled my head on a spike protruding from the ceiling, the result of a construction error. Blood began pouring from the wound, and I was immediately thrust into a life-threatening situation.*
>
> *In that critical moment, intuition kicked in, drawing on knowledge and experiences accumulated over the years. A memory from a fifth-grade health class resurfaced, reminding me to "apply pressure to the wound immediately and call 911!" I swiftly grabbed a nearby white hoodie that just happened to be on the floor next to me (divine intervention?) to staunch the bleeding and instructed one of my guests to guide the ambulance to my hard-to-find location, recalling a previous incident when the ambulance missed the turn from the main road to the private driveway.*
>
> *While waiting for help, I distinctly recall recognizing that I was in a fight-or-flight mode, a topic I had recently attended a seminar about. How interesting, I thought; if I make it through this, I will be able to tell this story at the next lecture! My intuition guided me to make the right decisions, ensuring that help arrived promptly. With quick treatment and 16 stitches, I eventually recovered from the accident.*

This experience demonstrates the power of intuition in emergency decision-making. When faced with high-stress situations, our intuition can help us make quick and effective decisions based on our past experiences and knowledge. In such moments, intuition can complement logic, allowing us to navigate challenging circumstances and emerge safely on the other side.

Creative Problem Solving with Intuition

In scenarios requiring innovative thinking and problem-solving, intuition can help us break through mental barriers and find unique solutions. In these cases, intuition can spark an idea, while logical reasoning can help us refine and evaluate the idea's feasibility.

> *Personally, my best intuitive ideas often emerge after a good night's sleep. It's said that dreams can be our mind's way of working through problems, and I find that upon waking, I'm brimming with creative solutions. The only catch? I have to jot them down quickly before they vanish into the ether!*

> *Meditation is another fruitful source of inspiration for me. As I let my thoughts drift away, it's as if solutions materialize out of thin air. And just when I think I've stumbled upon the perfect answer, an even better one appears as if by magic.*

> *But perhaps the most curious setting for my eureka moments is the shower. For reasons unknown, my greatest ideas seem to strike amid the soothing spray of water. Unfortunately, this left me scrambling for a way to capture these fleeting thoughts — until I discovered the "Waterproof Idea Notepad"! Clearly, I wasn't the only one facing this peculiar predicament.*

Ultimately, the interplay between intuition and logic can help us tap into our creative problem-solving potential, transforming everyday settings like sleep, meditation, or even the shower into fertile ground for inspiration. Interspersed with some logic and a waterproof notepad, we can make the most of these moments when inspiration strikes.

Integrating Intuition into the Decision-Making Process

Integrating intuition into the decision-making process *may* provide valuable insights that complement a more logical, structured approach. My sense (yes, my intuition) is that it is best injected at the end when you have more experience and expertise in the subject matter of the decision. However, it is wise for one to consider how intuition can be incorporated mindfully at various stages of the process. By mindfully, I mean one should consciously step back *after* the logical process has been completed and then let the subconscious mind do its thing. Just sit back, quietly reflect on the process, and ask your mind, "Did I miss anything here?" By incorporating intuition at different stages of the decision-making process, you can create a more balanced and comprehensive approach that takes advantage of both your rational thinking and your instincts.

For example, during the evaluation phase, applying intuition can be helpful in determining if any critical factors have been overlooked or if any criteria need to be adjusted. For instance, after you have completed the "logical" System 1 thinking, you may meditate a bit on it and then *feel* that a particular criterion should be given more weight based on your experience. Then ask why that makes logical sense. If it does, then use it. If it doesn't, then feel free to discard it as there are potential emotional and cognitive biases at play.

Example

In the house purchase example, let's imagine that Option A ranked highest after a thorough, logical analysis based on objective criteria such as location, size, price, and amenities. However, when considering your intuitive feelings about the decision, you are drawn to Option B, which ranked lower in the logical evaluation.

This discrepancy between the logic-based score and your intuition creates a dilemma, leading to cognitive dissonance.

To resolve this cognitive dissonance, it's essential to reevaluate the decision-making process, considering both the logical analysis and the intuitive insights. This may involve reassessing the weighting of certain criteria, incorporating additional factors such as personal values or emotional connection to the property, or exploring potential biases in the analysis.

For example, you may realize that the emotional connection to Option B is due to its proximity to your family or the sentimental value of the neighborhood, factors that were not explicitly considered in the initial logical analysis. By incorporating these additional criteria and adjusting the weightings accordingly, you can achieve a more comprehensive and holistic evaluation that aligns with both your logical and intuitive preferences.

If you can resolve the cognitive dissonance by integrating both rational and intuitive perspectives into the decision-making process, you may begin to experience a tremendous amount of conviction in your final choice, and you are now ready to purchase the house of your dreams with conviction! If you are not able to reconcile the two, then you will need to decide whether to trust your gut or go with logic — not a wonderful place to be in, so it is important to put maximum effort into this final step in order to reconcile any differences.

Conclusion

Embarking on a decision-making journey, you have navigated the stages of criteria identification, options exploration, and scoring through a systematic and deliberate approach. In doing so, you've honed your subconscious mind, rapidly accumulating expertise and experience relevant to the decision at hand. This invaluable knowledge enhances your intuitive abilities, tailored to this specific decision.

By immersing yourself in the intricacies of your decision, your subconscious mind absorbs and processes the pertinent information, fostering a refined intuition grounded in a deeper comprehension of the decision's factors. Engaging in this comprehensive decision-making process effectively accelerates your mastery and experience in the subject matter.

Incorporating your intuition as a final step in decision making is fitting, but it shouldn't be the foundation of the process. Rather, start with logic and structured reasoning. As you progress, you may find that you draw on intuition earlier in the process. Upon completing the process, take a moment to reflect on your intuition. Should it conflict with your logical analysis, delve into the reasons for the discrepancy to resolve any cognitive dissonance. By identifying and addressing the missing elements, your logical and intuitive minds can help you reach a unified conclusion.

By melding logic and intuition in your decision-making strategy, you cultivate a balanced and comprehensive perspective. This fusion allows you to draw from the insights of structured analysis while heeding the subtle cues detected by your intuition. As a result, you're well-equipped to make informed, satisfying decisions with true conviction.

Summary

1. Intuition plays a crucial role in the decision-making process.
2. Integrating intuition with logical analysis can lead to a more comprehensive and balanced decision.
3. Gut feelings can highlight discrepancies or areas that need further investigation.
4. Cognitive dissonance can impact decision-making and should be addressed.
5. Intuition can help you identify inconsistencies or gaps in the decision-making process.
6. Steve Jobs and Warren Buffett relied on their intuition to make wise decisions.
7. Intuition can complement logic in emergency decision-making situations.
8. Intuition can drive you toward creative problem-solving.
9. Mindfully incorporating intuition at different stages of the decision-making process can lead to better outcomes.
10. Drawing on your intuition and applying logic in a decision-making process can lead you to make more informed decisions.

Questions

1. What is cognitive dissonance?

   Mental discomfort that arises when one holds two or more contradictory beliefs, values, or attitudes simultaneously.

2. How can intuition complement logic in decision-making?

   It draws on past experiences to make quick, effective decisions.

3. How did Warren Buffett use intuition with investments?

   He trusted his gut while using rigorous analysis and research to evaluate investments.

4. How can integrating intuition into the decision-making process lead to better outcomes?

   It can lead to a more comprehensive and balanced decision.

5. When should intuition be used in the decision-making process?

   In the end, when you have more expertise in the subject matter.

6. How can cognitive dissonance be addressed?

   By re-examining criteria, weighting, or assumptions.

7. What is the interplay between intuition and logic?

   Intuition sparks ideas, while logical helps evaluate feasibility.

8. What are the potential benefits of mindfully incorporating intuition at different stages of the decision-making process?

   It helps you identify critical factors that may have been.

9. How can intuition be helpful during the evaluation phase?

   It can help determine if any critical factors have been.

10. What is the relationship between intuition and cognitive biases?

    Intuition can be clouded by emotions and cognitive biases.

Exercises

1. Think of a past decision you made based on intuition alone. Then, reflect on the outcome and consider if incorporating more logic and analysis could have led to a better outcome.

2. Identify a current decision you need to make and create a decision matrix using both objective criteria and your intuition. Evaluate and compare your options based on both sets of criteria.

3. Practice mindfulness meditation for 5 to 10 minutes each day to help you tune into your intuition and inner wisdom. Before making a decision, take a few deep breaths and try to tap into your intuitive insights.

4. Imagine a scenario where your intuition and logic are in conflict. Write down the pros and cons of each option and try to identify the underlying reasons for your intuition.

5. Reflect on a time when you ignored your intuition and regretted it. Consider how you can use this experience to better incorporate intuition into future decision-making.

6. Brainstorm creative solutions to a problem without worrying about feasibility at first. Then, after generating a list of ideas, evaluate and refine them using logic and analysis.

7. Consider a decision that you have made purely based on logic and analysis. Reflect on whether incorporating intuition could have led to a more satisfying outcome.

8. Take note of any physical sensations or emotions that arise when considering different options in a decision. Use these as clues to tap into your intuition and guide your decision-making process.

9. Choose a decision you have made in the past and evaluate how much weight you gave to intuition versus logic. Consider whether rebalancing this approach could lead to better decision-making in the future.

10. Use active listening and tune into your intuition during discussions with others. Consider how your intuitive insights can complement or challenge others' logical arguments.

Principle 9

Decide with Conviction

"Once you make a decision, the universe conspires to make it happen."
- Ralph Waldo Emerson

Move Forward by Adapting and Refining Your Skills

Deciding with conviction when logic and intuition align will allow you to have confidence in your decisions, giving you a clear sense of purpose and a potential path of action you can take. This sense of purpose can be especially valuable when facing complex or high-stakes decisions.

Key Question
How can we confidently take action on our decisions, learn from the outcomes, and continuously improve our decision-making process for future choices?

In the world of decision-making, conviction is king. It is the foundation upon which effective decisions are made and executed. However, developing conviction can be challenging, especially when logic and intuition are not aligned. In this chapter, we will explore the importance of conviction in decision-making and the role adaptability and continuous improvement play in ensuring that decisions remain effective and relevant.

By aligning logic and intuition, cultivating conviction, and remaining adaptable, you can make better decisions and achieve greater success in life and business. A study published in the Journal of Behavioral Decision-making found that the most effective decision-makers use intuition and logic. In addition, the study found that intuition or logic alone can lead to biased or incomplete decisions. However, combining intuition and logic can help decision-makers make more accurate and effective decisions.[34] There is no better feeling than the feeling you get when you have rock-solid confidence on a matter you have been struggling with. You now know the way forward with 100% certainty and confidence! However, getting to a level of conviction can be challenging, especially in situations when multiple variables and stakeholders are involved.

Additionally, adaptability and continuous improvement are crucial components of effective decision-making. They allow flexibility in response to changing circumstances and the ability to learn and grow from past decisions. By embracing these concepts, individuals and teams can make better decisions and achieve greater success in all areas of life.

The Importance of Conviction in Decision-Making

Aligning Logic and Intuition in Cultivating Conviction

Logic and intuition, as you now know, are both essential components of decision-making. Logic provides a rational framework for decision-making, while intuition provides insight from the subconscious mind. To cultivate conviction, it is essential that both are aligned because then and only then does decision-making become more effective and efficient.

When logic and intuition are not aligned, decision-making can become challenging. If you've ever made a decision solely "by the book" or, likewise, just because it "felt good," then you understand that decisions made purely with logic without taking intuition into account may lack creativity or innovation. On the

---

[34] Dane, E., & Pratt, M. G. (2007). Exploring intuition and its role in managerial decision making. Journal of Behavioral Decision Making, 20(1), 1-21. doi:10.1002/bdm.544

other hand, those decisions made purely with intuition and without any logical reasoning may lack substance or practicality.

The key is to find the right balance between logic and intuition so that the decision is well-informed and feels right.

The Difference between Conviction and Moving Forward Tentatively without Certainty

As we discussed, conviction is built on the alignment of logic and intuition, providing a solid foundation for decision-making. When you have conviction, you have confidence in your decision and are willing to take risks to achieve your desired outcome. Conviction allows you to move forward with purpose and clarity, even in the face of uncertainty or opposition. Having conviction provides you with confidence in making decisions and helps you overcome the challenges and obstacles bound to arise during execution. When you have conviction in your decision, you are more likely to remain committed and motivated, even when faced with adversity. Conviction provides a sense of purpose and direction, which can help you to stay focused and determined in the face of setbacks or obstacles. You are on a mission!

On the other hand, moving forward tentatively without certainty is a recipe for indecision and hesitancy. When unsure about a decision, you may second-guess yourself and delay taking action. This delay in action can lead to missed opportunities, wasted resources, and, ultimately, a lack of progress. In some cases, moving forward tentatively without conviction can even result in making the wrong decision, as you may be swayed by the opinions of others or external factors.

Having conviction can also inspire others to believe in your idea and support you in its execution. When you are confident and passionate about your decision, you can communicate its importance and value to others more effectively, motivating them to work alongside you toward achieving the desired outcome. This can result in a more cohesive team, greater collaboration, and increased success in executing the decision.

That said, one of the biggest challenges in decision-making is when not all team members share a point of conviction. In situations where team members disagree or are uncertain about a decision, it can be difficult to move forward. However, practicing the principle of "disagree and commit" is essential even when not everyone shares your conviction. This means that team members should voice their concerns and provide feedback but ultimately commit to the decision made by the group.

Real-life Examples of Decision-Making with and without Aligned Logic and Intuition

Here are real-life examples of decision-making that illustrate the importance of finding the right balance of logic and intuition.

> *The story of the creation of the Post-it® Note by 3M is a well-known example of the importance of intuition in decision-making. As mentioned, the Post-it Note was created accidentally during a failed attempt to create a super-strong adhesive. However, according to Gary Klein's article in the* Harvard Business Review, *the creators of the Post-it Note were able to recognize the potential of their accidental invention through intuition.*

> *Klein explains that the creators of the Post-it Note, Spencer Silver, and Art Fry, were both familiar with the properties of the adhesive they were working with. They had a hunch that the adhesive could be used to create a new kind of product, despite the fact that it had failed to meet the original goal of creating a super-strong adhesive. Their intuition led them to experiment with the adhesive, eventually creating the now-iconic Post-it Note.*

> *The Post-it Note is just one example of the power of intuition in decision-making. As Klein notes, intuition can be particularly useful in situations where there is incomplete or ambiguous information. In these situations, intuition can help decision-makers to recognize patterns and connections that might not be immediately apparent through logical analysis alone.*

The story of the creation of the Post-it note is a powerful reminder of the importance of intuition in decision-making. By remaining open to their intuition and willingness to experiment, Spencer Silver and Art Fry were able to turn a failed experiment into a hugely successful product.[35]

Conviction in the Investment World

I vividly recall an important discussion I had with John, the co-founder and portfolio manager of our hedge fund. He asked for a meeting, closed the door, and said, "Rich, I need your help. I need some type of process to figure out the conviction level of our analysts when they pitch me an idea for the portfolio."

He gave me an example where one of the senior members of the team, also a portfolio manager, pitched John a macro idea. When he finished the pitch, he jumped up, pounded John's desk, and said, "I am positive of this. I have never been more positive about anything in my life! We must move on this!"

John said, "Rich, that is the type of conviction I am looking for. The trouble is that analysts have different personalities, so it is hard to read their level of conviction." (By the way, the conviction level was spot on for this investment.)

John is one of the most, if not the most, intelligent people I have ever met, and I learned many decision lessons from him. In fact, he is so passionate about the topic of making quality decisions that he taught an entire course on it at the University of Virginia. As a portfolio manager, he was looking for the conviction level of those who recommended ideas to him as one piece of the puzzle — one large piece. The second piece was, of course, his own level of conviction. Once he had both, then the sky was the limit.

With John's guidance, I embarked right away on designing a scoring system for each position in our portfolio utilizing the process we discussed in this book. This score would, at a

---

[35] Source: "The Power of Intuition in Decision Making" by Gary Klein, *Harvard Business Review*, June 2003.

minimum, indicate the level of logical confidence that an analyst or portfolio manager had in the idea and would provide John with a consistent basis for a decision. If they followed the last step in the process to align intuition and logic, then the score would contain both. Of course, the missing part was the emotion with which an analyst presented an idea. That's a big indication of the level of conviction somebody has. The "pounding the table" was certainly expressed with emotion.

Steve Jobs' Level of Conviction on the iPhone

The story of Apple's Steve Jobs and the creation of the iPhone[36] is a prime example of the power of conviction in decision-making.

Jobs was convinced that the iPhone would revolutionize the smartphone industry and change how people interacted with technology. Despite initial skepticism from consumers and industry experts, Jobs remained committed to his vision and was willing to take significant risks to make it a reality.

One of the biggest challenges that Jobs faced was the issue of limited wireless network coverage. At the time, wireless networks were not equipped to handle the data demands of the iPhone, and many carriers were hesitant to invest in the necessary infrastructure upgrades. However, Jobs remained convinced that the iPhone was the future of mobile technology and continued to push forward with its development.

Through his conviction and confidence in the decision-making process, Jobs overcame these challenges and ushered in a new era of mobile technology. The iPhone revolutionized the smartphone industry, paving the way for the development of other cutting-edge technologies, such as mobile apps, digital assistants, and mobile payments.

---

[36] Source: Vance, A. (2015). Elon Musk: Tesla, SpaceX, and the quest for a fantastic future. HarperCollins.

This example highlights the importance of conviction in decision-making and the role it can play in helping us overcome challenges and obstacles. With conviction, individuals and teams can remain committed to their vision and goals, even when faced with significant challenges or opposition.

Adaptability

It is important to note that conviction does not mean being rigid or inflexible. Rather, it is the ability to adapt and refine your decision-making process while maintaining the confidence that you are moving in the right direction. Conviction allows you to be decisive and take action while remaining open to feedback and adjusting course when necessary.

Adaptability is a vital leadership skill that extends beyond the realm of decision-making because it holds immense significance in life and business. As highlighted in Charles Darwin's legendary book *On the Origin of Species*, adaptability is cited as the number one trait necessary for thriving in any environment — and it is even more critical in today's ever-changing world.[37] In life, adaptability allows individuals to navigate personal challenges, transitions, and new situations with resilience and confidence, leading to greater overall well-being. In business, adaptability is the key to staying competitive, as companies must continually evolve and innovate to keep up with shifting market demands and industry trends. Leaders who embrace adaptability can better steer their organizations through uncertainty, seize emerging opportunities, and foster a culture of continuous learning and growth. The bottom line is to adapt and thrive. If you aren't able to adapt, you die. That's how important this is.

It's important to note that there can often be pushback from others, including team members, when adaptability is being practiced. This is because adaptability usually involves change

---

[37] Darwin, C. (1859). On the Origin of Species by Means of Natural Selection, or the Preservation of Favoured Races in the Struggle for Life. John Murray.

— and change often requires effort and resources. It may mean learning new skills, adapting to new processes or systems, or reallocating resources differently. This can be time-consuming, and it may take a while for people to adjust to the new way of doing things. Change can also be uncomfortable and disruptive. People generally prefer stability and predictability, and when something disrupts that, it can create stress and anxiety, especially if the change is sudden or unexpected.

In many cases, the more advance notice you can give, the better reaction you may see. People may resist change if they feel their roles or status within the team or organization are threatened. Likewise, if the change involves a shift in responsibilities or a redistribution of power, some individuals may feel like they are losing something or being left behind.

To overcome pushback and encourage adaptability, it is essential to communicate the benefits of the change clearly, involve team members in the decision-making process, provide support and resources to help with the transition, and recognize and reward those who can adapt and succeed in the new environment. Despite the challenges, adaptability is crucial for success in today's fast-paced, ever-changing world.

Staying Open to New Information

The concept of adaptability in decision-making means emphasizing the importance of staying open to new information, knowing when to re-evaluate decisions, and being flexible in response to changing circumstances. By cultivating adaptability, you can ensure that your decisions remain effective and relevant even when faced with unforeseen challenges or new information. Through real-life examples, we will illustrate the value of adaptability in various scenarios and demonstrate how being flexible and open to change can lead to better overall outcomes.

While committing to a decision is crucial, it's also important to remain receptive to new information and be prepared to make changes if circumstances require it. Flexibility can help you adapt to changing circumstances and make more effective decisions.

Knowing When to Re-evaluate Decisions

Sometimes, new information or changing circumstances may warrant re-evaluating your initial decision. Recognize when it's appropriate to revisit a choice and be willing to adjust your path accordingly.

> *At Arootah, we have a large team of coaches and advisors who work hard to support our clients in their decision-making process. We know that technology plays a big role in our client's success, so we invest a lot of time and resources into developing our decision-making app. But even with the best intentions, we don't always get it right on the first try. That's where our focus groups come in. We bring in a diverse group of individuals, coaches, and advisors to test out our app and provide us with feedback. We avoid being defensive, as we know that this feedback is valuable. Instead, we take the time to evaluate the feedback and make significant changes to our app expediently, if necessary. Thanks to our adaptability and willingness to change, we can quickly make the necessary adjustments and improve our app — and we end up with a product that is even better than we had initially envisioned.*

Continuous Improvement in Decision-Making

Decision-making is not a static process. It is an ongoing practice that requires continuous improvement. There are many ways to improve decision-making skills; the most important one you are doing now is reading my book!

Below, I offer three other ways to improve decision-making skills: learning from past decisions, refining decision-making models, and providing a hypothetical example of improving talent acquisition processes for a business.

Learning from Past Decisions

Reflecting on previous decisions and their outcomes can help you learn valuable lessons and improve your decision-making skills. Analyze both successful *and* unsuccessful choices to gain insight for future decisions. It's important to do both. When analyzing what went right with a successful decision, not only do you want to do more of that, but you also want to get better at that part of the decision-making process as well. When analyzing decisions that were wrong during this postmortem, it is a good idea to figure out if the process or model was wrong, if it was a user error, or if it was just plain old bad luck. The key question here is: *Would you have made the same decision again, given the same set of facts?* If the answer is yes, the decision model likely was fine all along, and there is no need to change it. However, if you identify a model flaw, change it immediately. A criterion may not have had the proper weighting, or you may have missed a criterion completely.

Refining Decision-Making Models

Failing to change your decision-making models based on new information is akin to Albert Einstein's famous quote: "Insanity is doing the same thing over and over and expecting different results." Use your experiences to refine and improve your decision-making models. Identify any gaps or weaknesses in your current approach and make adjustments to enhance the decision-making process.

In addition to using past experiences to refine and improve your decision-making models, it's also important to continuously seek new information and perspectives, as noted previously. This can be achieved by engaging in ongoing learning and professional development opportunities, such as attending workshops or training sessions, reading relevant literature, or seeking mentorship or coaching.

Another way to refine decision-making models is to incorporate diverse viewpoints and input from others. This is akin to challenging the criteria assumptions noted in our process. This can be achieved through collaboration with colleagues or seeking out feedback from stakeholders. By involving others in the decision-making process, you can gain valuable insights and perspectives that may have otherwise been overlooked.

We take great pride in our talent acquisition process at Arootah. We use the decision matrix heavily, and we update the model whenever we learn something new. For instance, we learned that the second comparison measurement was missing when we stumbled upon it one day when collaboratively reviewing candidates for a position. It occurred to me that we needed to focus just on ranking them against each other and not so much on the scores. The initial scores had just served to filter out the candidates that didn't make the cut. Now we had the finalists, and we needed to rank them against each other for each category. We would then still apply the weighting to each to come up with the final score.

It's essential to regularly assess the effectiveness of your decision-making models and adjust as needed. This may involve conducting regular audits or evaluations to identify areas for improvement or seeking out feedback from stakeholders to ensure that the decision-making process meets their needs and expectations. By regularly refining and updating your decision-making models, you can ensure that they remain effective and relevant over time.

House Example: Decisiveness and Continual Improvement

Let's apply this framework to our hypothetical house purchase example.

Committing to the Chosen House

Once you have completed the decision-making process and selected a house, it's crucial to take decisive action by making an offer and moving forward with the purchase.

Re-evaluating the Decision if New Information Arises

If new information comes to light, such as a previously undisclosed issue with the property, be open to re-evaluating your choice and considering other options.

Reflect on the house-buying process and identify any areas where your decision-making model could be improved. Then, use these insights to make more informed decisions in future house purchases.

Conclusion

This chapter emphasizes the importance of conviction in decision-making and how it is the foundation of *effective* decision-making. Conviction is built on the alignment of logic and intuition, and it allows for decisive action and the achievement of desired outcomes. The difference between conviction and moving forward tentatively without certainty is crucial, and moving forward with conviction can inspire others to support and believe in the decision. Real-life examples of decision-making with aligned and misaligned logic and intuition are highlighted, including the story of the creation of the Post-it Note by 3M and the conviction of Steve Jobs in creating the iPhone. Adaptability and continuous improvement are also crucial components of effective decision-making, allowing individuals and teams to remain open to new information, re-evaluate decisions when necessary, and refine decision-making models over time. By embracing these concepts, individuals and teams can make better decisions and achieve greater success in all areas of life.

Summary

1. Conviction is essential for effective decision-making.
2. Aligning logic and intuition is key to cultivating conviction.
3. Moving forward with conviction allows for decisive action and the achievement of desired outcomes.
4. Conviction can inspire others to support and believe in a decision.
5. Real-life examples illustrate the importance of finding the right balance between logic and intuition.
6. Adaptability is a vital leadership skill that allows for course correction when necessary.
7. Staying open to new information and re-evaluating decisions when needed is essential.
8. Continuous improvement is necessary for effective decision-making.
9. Learning from past decisions and incorporating diverse viewpoints can improve decision-making models.
10. Conviction, adaptability, and continuous improvement are all necessary components of successful decision-making in all areas of life.

Questions

1. Why is it important to decide with conviction when logic and intuition align?

    It allows you to make decisions confidently.

2. How can we act with conviction on our decisions?

    It requires aligning both logic and intuition.

3. What is the difference between moving forward with conviction and moving forward tentatively without certainty?

    Moving forward with conviction means having confidence in your decision, while moving forward tentatively can lead to missed opportunities and suboptimal outcomes.

4. What is the role of adaptability in decision-making?

    It allows us to refine our decision-making process.

5. How can we stay open to new information while committing to a decision?

    Flexibility can help you adapt to changing circumstances and make more effective decisions.

6. When should we re-evaluate our decisions?

    If new information is presented or circumstances change.

7. How can we continuously improve our decision-making process?

    By learning from past decisions and refining models.

8. What is the role of intuition in decision-making?

    It can help decision-makers recognize patterns and connections that might not be immediately apparent through logical analysis alone.

9. How can we cultivate conviction in decision-making?

    By aligning logic and intuition.

10. What are the benefits of having conviction in decision-making?

    It allows you to move forward confidently.

Exercises

1. Reflecting on a recent decision, consider if you aligned logic and intuition and moved forward with conviction or tentatively without certainty. Then, analyze how this impacted the outcome.

2. Practice the "disagree and commit" principle with a team member or colleague. Voice your concerns and provide feedback, but ultimately commit to the decision made by the group.

3. Seek feedback from a colleague or stakeholder on your decision and incorporate their perspective into your decision-making process.

4. Identify a decision-making model you use regularly and explore ways to refine it to incorporate diverse viewpoints.

5. Think of a challenging decision you made in the past and identify what you learned from it. Then, consider how you can apply that knowledge to future decisions.

6. Practice adaptability in your personal life by trying something new or navigating a challenging situation with resilience and flexibility.

7. Reflect on a past decision and consider how you could have adjusted your course given new information or changing circumstances.

8. Create a scoring system for decisions that considers logical confidence, intuition alignment, and emotional conviction, similar to the one mentioned in the chapter.

9. Identify a decision-making model used by your organization and brainstorm ways to refine it and incorporate diverse viewpoints.

10. Incorporate both logic and intuition in your decision-making process. Consider the facts and your gut feelings before arriving at a decision.

Principle 10

Collaborate for Consensus

"Collaboration allows teachers to capture each other's fund of collective intelligence."

- Mike Schmoker

Refining and Aligning Diverse Perspectives for Optimal Results

Collaborating for consensus is a valuable approach to decision-making in a group setting, as it allows for diverse perspectives and expertise to be considered. By encouraging everyone to participate and share their opinions, a mutually agreed-upon decision can be reached that reflects the needs and perspectives of all involved. This approach can lead to better decision outcomes, improved team dynamics, and increased buy-in and commitment from stakeholders.

Key Question
How can we leverage diverse perspectives to collaborate effectively, make decisions, reach a consensus, and achieve optimal results?

Collaboration enhances individual decision-making skills and is a key component of effective group decision-making. In this chapter, we will explore the benefits of collaboration and provide a guide for how to collaborate effectively for consensus.

Collaborating with others can provide a wealth of knowledge, experience, and perspectives that can improve the quality of decision-making. However, collaboration can also present challenges like conflicting opinions, differing priorities, and communication barriers. By learning effective collaboration techniques, groups can overcome these challenges and work towards achieving optimal results.

The key principles of effective group decision-making include communication, active listening, and conflict resolution. In this chapter, we will explore strategies for building a consensus, such as brainstorming, ranking, and voting. We will also discuss the importance of maintaining open-mindedness, flexibility, and a willingness to compromise to achieve the best possible outcome.

Preparing for Group Decision-Making

Before any group decision-making can take place, it is essential to prepare the team for effective collaboration. This involves building a diverse team, setting clear goals and objectives, and establishing clear roles and responsibilities for each group member.

Thought particle: The accuracy of the group decision is an important statistic. Research has shown that groups can make more accurate decisions than individuals, especially if the group is diverse and includes members with different perspectives and expertise.[38]

Build a Diverse Team

A diverse team is crucial for effective collaboration. By bringing together people with different backgrounds, experiences, and perspectives, the group can benefit from a wider range of ideas and solutions. It is essential to ensure that the team is not too

---

[38]

Gomez L. E. & Bernet P. (n.d.). Diversity improves performance and outcomes. *Journal of the National Medical Association* (383–392). https://doi.org/10.1016/j.jnma.2019.01.006

homogenous, as this can lead to "groupthink" and limit the group's ability to consider different perspectives. Building a diverse team can be a challenging task, but it is essential for effective collaboration and decision-making.

There are several strategies one can use to build a diverse team:

1.   Skills Identification
Begin by identifying the skills and experience needed to achieve the goals of the decision-making process. This will help to identify the types of people who should be part of the team.

2.   Sourcing Strategy
Rather than relying on the same pool of people that have been used in the past, create a strategy to look to new sources. This may involve seeking out people from different departments or even different organizations.

3.   Diversity Goals
Set specific diversity goals for the team, such as the percentage of women or people from underrepresented groups that should be included in decision-making processes. Be sure to choose the most qualified person for the role, though.

4.   Referrals
Encourage team members to refer people they know who have the necessary skills and experience but may be outside the usual pool of candidates.

5.   Blind Hiring
Blind hiring practices involve removing identifying information, such as name and gender, from resumes and applications. This can help eliminate bias and ensure that all candidates are evaluated solely on their skills and experience.

6.   Inclusivity Culture
Creating an inclusive culture within the team is necessary because it ensures that everyone feels valued and respected. This involves promoting open communication, encouraging different

perspectives, and actively addressing any biases or stereotypes that may arise.

Set Clear Goals, Assign Roles, and Design Plans

1. Setting Clear Goals

Setting clear goals and objectives is essential for successful group decision-making. The team should clearly understand what they are trying to achieve and what outcomes they are working towards. This helps to keep the group focused and on track and allows them to measure their progress toward their goals.

2. Establishing Clear Roles and Responsibilities

Establishing clear roles and responsibilities for each group member is also important for effective collaboration. This helps group members avoid confusion and misunderstandings and ensures everyone is clear on what they are expected to contribute to the decision-making process. In addition, each team member should understand their strengths and weaknesses and how they can best contribute to the group.

3. Designing Plans

Designing plans is another key element of preparing for group decision-making. This involves creating a roadmap or strategy that outlines the steps the team will take to achieve their goals. The plan should include specific action items, timelines, and milestones to ensure the team is making progress toward the desired outcome. It should also be flexible enough to allow for adjustments as needed based on new information or changing circumstances.

When designing plans, it is important to involve the *entire team* in the process. This helps to ensure that everyone has a voice in shaping the plan and that it reflects the perspectives and experiences of the entire group. It also helps build buy-in and commitment from the team, as they are more likely to be invested in a plan they helped create.

By setting clear goals, assigning roles, and designing plans, the team can be better prepared for effective collaboration and decision-making. This lays the foundation for success by ensuring everyone is on the same page and working towards the same objectives.

Collaborating for Consensus

Once the team is prepared, the group can move on to the collaborative decision-making process. The goal of the collaboration is to ensure that everyone's voice is heard and that the group can work towards a consensus decision that everyone can support. Here are a few steps that can be taken to ensure that the culture for collaboration is set.

1. Identify and Understand Different Perspectives

The team should be encouraged to share their thoughts and ideas openly and to listen actively to the perspectives of others. This helps to ensure that all perspectives are considered and that the group can work towards a decision that considers and factors before the group makes .

2. Encourage Open Communication and Active Listening

Open communication and active listening create an environment where team members feel comfortable sharing their opinions and ideas without fear of judgment or reprisal. Active listening involves truly hearing what others say and considering their perspectives before responding. This helps to ensure that all voices are heard. In addition, the group can work toward a decision that reflects the views of everyone involved.

3. Navigate Conflicts and Disagreements

It is important to address conflicts openly and constructively and work towards a resolution everyone can support. This involves acknowledging and respecting the views of all team members and finding common ground where possible.

Refining and Aligning Diverse Perspectives

After the group has considered all relevant perspectives, it is important to refine and align these perspectives toward a shared goal. This involves identifying areas of agreement and disagreement within the group, working to find common ground, and aligning perspectives toward a shared goal.

1. Identifying Areas of Agreement and Disagreement

Identifying areas of agreement and disagreement within the group involves synthesizing the diverse perspectives that have been shared. This helps the group identify areas of overlap and consensus and areas where further discussion is needed.

To identify areas of alignment and misalignment, the group can create a list of points of agreement and disagreement based on the different perspectives shared. Then, by summarizing the main points of each perspective and comparing them, the group can identify areas of agreement and areas where further discussion or clarification is needed.

2. Finding Common Ground

Working to find common ground and aligning perspectives towards a shared goal involves finding ways to bridge any gaps between different perspectives. This may involve compromise or creative solutions that require the team to consider all members' concerns and priorities.

To establish a shared understanding, the group can explore approaches to identify commonalities that exist between different perspectives. One way to do this is to identify shared values or priorities everyone can agree on and build on those to find a mutually beneficial solution. It may also involve brainstorming and exploring creative solutions that incorporate the perspectives and input of all team members.

3. Aligning Perspectives

Making informed decisions by synthesizing diverse perspectives and feedback involves using the insights gained from collaboration to make a well-informed decision that reflects the views of everyone involved. This ensures that the decision is effective and equitable and everyone feels invested in its success.

To align perspectives, the group can use the insights gained from collaboration to make a well-informed decision that reflects the views of everyone involved. This may involve synthesizing the different perspectives into a single proposal that integrates the various viewpoints and input of team members. It may also include using techniques such as voting or ranking to prioritize different options and arrive at a final decision everyone can support.

> *Collaboration is like a secret weapon in the world of decision-making, and it's one that's often overlooked. At both Blue Ridge Capital and Arootah, I have found over the years that decisions made in collaboration are usually of a much higher quality. For instance, our Talent Acquisition Process involves various touchpoints with candidates. We initially score them individually, and then we get together for the comparative step in the process. The diverse viewpoints always lead to significant insights about the candidates, leading to better-informed decisions. In this way, we arrive at the best score for each candidate.*

> *And when it comes to committees, I'm definitely a fan. The committees tasked with making a decision can work together collaboratively to arrive at a better decision than the lone wolf ever could! It's like having a team of superheroes taking on a challenge together. Everyone has their strengths, and together they can overcome any obstacle. So, don't be afraid to embrace collaboration and leverage the power of diverse perspectives to make the best decisions possible.*

Conclusion

Effective collaboration is essential for making decisions in groups, as it allows organizations to leverage their members' collective intelligence and diverse perspectives to arrive at well-informed decisions that reflect the views and priorities of all team members. The key principles of effective group decision-making include communication, active listening, conflict resolution, strategies for building consensus, and aligning perspectives toward a shared goal. By following these principles and strategies, teams can overcome the challenges of group decision-making and achieve optimal results. To enhance your effectiveness as a leader or team member, apply these principles in your decision-making processes and continue developing your collaboration and consensus-building skills.

Summary

1. Collaboration is an essential component of effective decision-making in groups.

2. Effective collaboration involves building a diverse team, setting clear goals and objectives, and establishing clear roles and responsibilities for each group member.

3. The key principles of effective group decision-making include communication, active listening, and conflict resolution.

4. Strategies for building consensus include brainstorming, ranking, and voting.

5. Open-mindedness, flexibility, and a willingness to compromise are important for achieving optimal results.

6. Identifying areas of agreement and disagreement, finding common ground, and aligning perspectives toward a shared goal are important for refining and aligning diverse perspectives.

7. Creating an inclusive culture within the team is essential for ensuring that everyone feels valued and respected.

8. Active listening involves truly hearing what others say and considering their perspectives before responding.

9. It is important to address conflicts openly and constructively and work towards a resolution everyone can support.

10. By following these principles, teams can navigate the challenges of group decision-making and arrive at well-informed decisions that achieve optimal results.

Questions

1. What is the key component of effective decision-making in groups?

    Collaboration.

2. What are the challenges that collaboration can present?

    Conflicting opinions, priorities, and communication barriers.

3. What are key principles of effective group decision-making?

    Communication, active listening, and conflict resolution.

4. What are some strategies for building consensus?

    Brainstorming, ranking, and voting.

5. Why is open-mindedness important for achieving optimal results?

    It allows the group to consider different perspectives and find creative solutions.

6. How to refine and align diverse perspectives?

    Identifying areas of agreement and disagreement, finding common ground, and aligning perspectives towards a shared goal.

7. Why is creating an inclusive culture within the team important?

    It ensures that everyone feels valued and respected.

8. What is active listening?

    Active listening involves truly hearing what others say and considering their perspectives before responding.

9. How to address conflicts in group decision-making?

    Openly and constructively, the group should work towards a resolution that everyone can support.

10. What are the benefits of collaboration in decision-making?

    It provides a wealth of knowledge, experience, and perspectives that can improve the quality of decision-making.

Exercises

1. Identify a decision-making situation where collaboration could have improved the quality of the decision.
2. Brainstorm strategies for building a diverse team for a specific decision-making process.
3. Practice active listening in a conversation with a friend or colleague.
4. Research and analyze a real-life example of a group decision-making process that was successful due to collaboration.
5. Role-play a group decision-making scenario and practice conflict resolution techniques.
6. Conduct a survey to identify potential biases or stereotypes within your team and work toward addressing them.
7. Write a list of important values and priorities for your team to consider when making decisions.
8. Analyze a decision-making process in a fictional book or movie and identify where collaboration could have improved the outcome.
9. Practice designing plans for a hypothetical decision-making process involving the entire team.
10. Interview a successful leader or team member and ask them about their experience with effective collaboration and decision-making.

Principle 11

Set Yourself Up for Success with Keystone Decisions

*"If you focus on changing or cultivating keystone
habits, you can cause widespread shifts."*

- Charles Duhigg

Maximizing with a Domino Effect

Keystone decisions are critical decisions that have a significant
impact on other decisions. By identifying and prioritizing them,
individuals and teams can use their time and resources more
efficiently, avoid wasted efforts on less impactful decisions, and
increase the likelihood of achieving their objectives. This
principle helps you streamline the decision-making process and
ensures that you direct efforts toward the most crucial choices
and the most beneficial actions.

Key Question

*How can we set ourselves up for success by making
strategic decisions that have positive downstream
effects on other decisions?*

In this chapter, we will explore the concept of keystone
decisions and their impact on other decisions. Certain decisions
act as a catalyst, setting off a chain reaction of other positive
decisions, ultimately contributing to our overall success.

We will closely examine some practical examples to illustrate this
concept. For instance, we will examine how something as simple
as changing your email address can significantly impact the
decisions you need to make. We will also explore how having a
set shopping list delivered to your door can streamline the
decision-making process when it comes to meal planning and

196 The Decision Principles

grocery shopping. Additionally, we will discuss how clothing decisions can set the tone for your day and impact your productivity and overall well-being.

By the end of this chapter, you will have a solid understanding of keystone decisions, and you will also have a few practical strategies for making smart keystone decisions that can set you up for success.

Changing my Email Address

At about ten in the morning, I was sitting at my desk, and I already had about 100 emails in my inbox. I'm one of those people who doesn't like to have unanswered emails at the end of the day, so let's just say this was causing me a little bit of stress, not to mention a lot of time on non-urgent and not-important tasks. I remember thinking that many of them were requests from people outside my firm asking me for something they knew I wouldn't be able to give them anyway. Many of these people I didn't know. There were subscriptions I had signed up for years ago that I mostly didn't read, and when I did, it wasn't a high return on my time.

Each email represented a decision that needed to be made: should I reply now, later, or not at all? All decisions require energy, so I was losing not only time but also mental energy. Decision fatigue! If I were to reply to even a small portion of them, this would take up an enormous amount of time. The more I thought about it, the more I realized that the sheer volume of emails made it harder for me to focus on the more important decisions I needed to make throughout the day.

Was I doomed to just have this inbox keep growing and growing? Then a light bulb went off.

I thought, "Why don't I just change my email address and then only give it to people that absolutely must have it?" I would start again fresh. Inbox of ZERO. Then I could consciously decide who I was OK receiving emails from. I would not even say anything to the others but would keep two email inboxes. Of course, when I mentioned to others on my team that I was contemplating doing this, the usual response was, "You can't do that! What if somebody important needs to find you!" Well, I didn't change my phone number or the number of the firm, so if somebody important needed to track me down about something important, they could certainly find me. Besides, my assistant and I could still check my other email occasionally.

So, I took a look at the pros and cons, which were clear, and made the decision to change my address. It was one of the smartest things I've ever done in terms of setting myself up for success.

The idea of **keystone decisions** came to me when I discovered the concept of **keystone habits**, which was introduced to me in Charles Duhigg's book *The Power of Habit*[39]. Duhigg explains how making one small change (*i.e.*, joining a gym) can lead to a cascade of positive outcomes in other areas (*i.e.*, better eating habits, a new social circle) of our lives. In my example, changing my email address was my keystone *decision* that led to hundreds of fewer decisions per day, which meant more time, more energy — and less stress.

This is the power of a keystone decision: it sets off a chain reaction of outcomes.

Choice Architecture

Choice Architecture, a term popularized in the book *Nudge* by Richard H. Thaler and Cass R. Sunstein[40], refers to the way in which options are presented to individuals that influence their decision-making without restricting their freedom to choose. By understanding how choice architecture works, we can help individuals make better keystone decisions.

---

[39] Duhigg, C. (2012). The Power of Habit: Why We Do What We Do in Life and Business. Random House.

[40] Thaler, R. H., & Sunstein, C. R. (2008). *Nudge: Improving decisions about health, wealth, and happiness.* Penguin.

The concept of choice architecture is closely linked to the idea of *nudges*, which are subtle interventions that guide people toward better choices while still maintaining their freedom to choose. Nudges rely on various techniques, such as defaults, framing, feedback, and incentives, to influence decision making in a non-coercive manner. By incorporating these techniques into the presentation of keystone decisions, we can encourage individuals to make choices that align with their long-term best interests and foster positive downstream effects on other decisions.

Defaults, for example, can be used to set options that are in the best interest of individuals, gently guiding them toward better decisions without eliminating their freedom to opt for other alternatives. **Framing** involves presenting options that highlights their benefits, potential losses, or long-term consequences, helping people resist the temptation of immediate gratification and choose options that better align with their long-term goals. **Feedback** plays a crucial role in helping individuals learn from their choices and make better decisions in the future. By providing timely and constructive feedback on the outcomes of certain decisions, we can help people become more aware of the long-term implications of their choices and develop a stronger resistance to immediate gratification. **Incentives** can be designed to reward long-term thinking and responsible decision-making, further counteracting the allure of immediate gratification.

More Keystone Decisions

Let's delve into various keystone decisions that can have a significant impact on your life and success. As we explore these keystone decisions, we will also point out the defaults, framing, feedback, and incentive techniques of each.

Keystone Decision: The Bedtime Decision

Getting sufficient sleep is by far the number one health decision you can make. It's more important than nutrition or exercise because it impacts just about every decision you make while you are awake. Therefore, deciding to set a boundary around a consistent bedtime can have a domino impact on several crucial decisions. For instance, it can positively impact your decision-making skills throughout the day because when you have a regular sleep routine, you are more likely to awaken feeling refreshed and energized, which can enhance your focus, concentration, and cognitive abilities. This can, in turn, help you make better decisions.

There is scientific evidence that sleep can improve decision-making. For example, a study published in the journal *Sleep* in 2017 found that sleep deprivation can impair decision-making processes while getting adequate sleep can improve decision-making abilities[41]. Another study published in the journal *Nature Communications* in 2019 found that sleep can help people to consolidate memories and integrate new information, which can improve decision-making abilities[42]. Likewise, one study published in the *Journal of Neuroscience*[43] found that sleep deprivation impairs the prefrontal cortex's ability to regulate the amygdala, a brain region responsible for processing emotions[44]. This can lead to more impulsive and emotionally driven decision-making.

For example, let's say I am sleep-deprived because I erroneously prioritized staying up late to do some work instead of getting a

---

[41] Killgore, W. D., Balkin, T. J., & Wesensten, N. J. (2017). Impaired decision making following 49 h of sleep deprivation. Sleep, 40(5), zsx056.

[42] Rasch, B., Büchel, C., Gais, S., & Born, J. (2019). Odor cues during slow-wave sleep prompt declarative memory consolidation. Nature Communications, 10(1), 1-11.

[43] Yoo, S. S., Gujar, N., Hu, P., Jolesz, F. A., & Walker, M. P. (2007). The human emotional brain without sleep--a prefrontal amygdala disconnect. Current Biology, 17(20), R877-8. doi: 10.1016/j.cub.2007.08.007

[44] Goldstein-Piekarski, A. N., Greer, S. M., Saletin, J. M., & Walker, M. P. (2015). Sleep deprivation impairs the human central and peripheral nervous system discrimination of social threat. Journal of Neuroscience, 35(28), 10135-10145.

good night's sleep. If I happen to be writing a book, as I am now, my efficiency and effectiveness will be lower, and any decisions I make will be of lower quality due to fatigue. Additionally, my ability to emotionally regulate and utilize the pause strategy necessary for sound leadership will be impaired.

The bottom line is that the decision to go to bed at the same time each night to get sufficient sleep is essential for regulating our emotions and making sound decisions, and by setting a *default* bedtime and *framing* it as a non-negotiable self-care routine, we gently push ourselves toward better sleep habits, which can lead to improved focus, concentration, and cognitive abilities throughout the day.

Keystone Decision: Decide What to Eat in Advance

When it comes to making healthy choices, one keystone decision that has worked wonders for many people is planning meals and grocery shopping in advance and avoiding grocery shopping when they are hungry! When we get hungry, our "immediate gratification" instincts kick in, and, for most of us, our healthy food choices don't stand a chance against those instincts. By designing a grocery list and planning your meals ahead of time, you can set yourself up for success by leaving no decision to make when it's time to eat; only healthy food is around to satisfy the cravings.

Eating well, like getting sufficient rest, has a domino effect on many other decisions. For example, if you eat a balanced and nutritious diet, you may be more likely to feel energized and motivated, which will lead you to knock down the exercise domino! When you prioritize your health and well-being through healthy eating habits, you may also be more likely to prioritize self-care in other ways, such as getting massages for stress relief. By the way, the converse is also true; if you make poor food choices and do not prioritize your health, you will be more likely to neglect other areas of your well-being. So, make the keystone decision to choose in advance what to eat before you are hungry and set yourself up for a positive, healthy domino effect.

Keystone Decision: You Can't Have Just One

Another keystone decision is what I refer to as You Can't Have Just One. What happens when you say you're going to have just one french fry or just one potato chip? You end up eating the whole bag! (And with the legalization of marijuana, you might even have another one!) The keystone decision is the choice of whether to even eat that first chip. It is much easier to avoid eating the first chip than resist the desire to eat a second one. This concept can also be applied to the bread often brought to the table at the beginning of a meal. It's tempting to indulge in just one little slice, but before you know it, the breadbasket is empty. To avoid this situation, I always politely tell the waiter "no thanks" and to please not put the bread on the table. By recognizing that it's easier to avoid eating the first unhealthy item, we create a default rule that helps us resist temptation.

Keystone Decision: What to Wear

Steve Jobs is a famous example of someone who made a keystone clothing decision by wearing his signature black turtleneck and jeans every day.[45] This reduced his decision fatigue score by freeing him from having to decide what to wear each day. It also simplified his clothing purchase decisions. This one decision allowed him to simplify his life and focus on more important decisions while still projecting a professional image. By establishing a default wardrobe, Jobs created a simple, professional image without expending additional time and energy on clothing choices.

Keystone Decision: How Much to Drink

Drinking alcohol can have far-reaching consequences, so making the decision to drink is a keystone decision. It can affect one's judgment, behavior, and overall well-being, potentially leading to a cascade of decisions with serious outcomes.

---

[45] Source: Isaacson, W. (2011). Steve Jobs. Simon & Schuster.

Moreover, it affects one's ability to make decisions effectively, leading to a lack of inhibition and impaired judgment. Therefore, it is crucial to make a thoughtful and deliberate decision about whether to drink, how much, and when to drink.

Alcohol consumption impairs decision-making abilities primarily by affecting System 2 (slow, deliberate) thinking. When under the influence of alcohol, the prefrontal cortex, which is associated with System 2 thinking, becomes impaired, resulting in a reduced ability to engage in conscious, deliberate decision-making processes. System 1 thinking is "unleashed," going unchecked by the rational, deliberate thinking of System 2, which has literally become impaired.

Additionally, alcohol consumption can also affect System 1 thinking by increasing one's likelihood of relying on biases and heuristics (mental shortcuts) in decision-making. This can lead to overconfidence in one's decision-making abilities and a tendency to ignore or dismiss important information.

Thus, alcohol consumption can impair System 1 and System 2 thinking, resulting in poor decision-making abilities that can lead to a cascade of other poor decisions. Some of the poor decisions that alcohol is often associated with are:

Unsafe Sex. One of the most common poor decisions associated with alcohol use is engaging in unsafe sex. Alcohol consumption can impair judgment and decision-making abilities, making it more difficult to make responsible choices regarding sexual behavior. This can increase the risk of unintended pregnancies, sexually transmitted infections, and other negative consequences.

Poor Financial Decisions. Alcohol use can also lead to poor financial decisions, as impaired judgment can lead to overspending or making poor investments. Additionally, repeated alcohol use can lead to addiction, which can have a wide range of negative effects on one's life, including financial difficulties, strained relationships, and reduced job performance.

Use of Drugs. Alcohol is often the trigger to taking illegal or prescription drugs for recreational purposes. Alcohol consumption can impair judgment and decision-making abilities, making it more likely for an individual to make poor choices, including experimenting with drugs or taking medications not prescribed to them. This can lead to negative consequences such as addiction, overdose, or legal troubles.

Drinking and Driving. This is another notorious decision that can result from alcohol consumption. When someone drinks alcohol, their ability to make sound judgments and their reaction time is impaired, which can result in them making the decision to drive while intoxicated. This is illegal and can lead to serious accidents, injuries, and even death.

The decision to drink alcohol can significantly affect one's life and well-being. It impairs decision-making abilities primarily by affecting System 2 thinking and increasing reliance on biases and heuristics in System 1 thinking. Therefore, it is crucial to make a deliberate and thoughtful decision about alcohol consumption, considering the potential consequences and impact on decision-making abilities. Implementing incentives and feedback mechanisms can help us manage alcohol consumption. By setting limits and rewarding ourselves for responsible drinking, we can avoid the negative consequences associated with excessive alcohol use, such as unsafe sex, poor financial decisions, drug use, and drinking and driving.

Keystone Decision: When to Say NO

When faced with peer pressure to take an action that you don't want to take, especially one that can lead to other negative decisions, deciding to say "no" is a keystone habit that can significantly impact an individual's life. It is an act of self-control and courage that can set the stage for making positive decisions in the future. Saying "no" requires an individual to resist the temptation of peer pressure, which can be especially challenging for young people.

Peer pressure is a powerful force that can influence an individual's decisions and actions. It is often exerted by friends or peers who encourage an individual to engage in behaviors that may not align with their values or goals. In the context of substance use, peer pressure can be a major factor in an individual's decision to smoke their first cigarette, start using an addictive, harmful drug, or drink alcohol irresponsibly (one can argue all drinking is irresponsible).

Saying "no" to peer pressure is the ultimate act of courage, as it requires an individual to stand up for their beliefs and values. It can be challenging to resist the pressure to fit in or be accepted by one's peers, but it is a necessary step in making healthy choices for oneself. By saying "no" to peer pressure, an individual can set themselves up for success by establishing boundaries and sticking to their goals.

In situations where an individual is faced with peer pressure, having a plan in place can be helpful. This may involve identifying potential triggers and developing strategies to avoid or manage them before facing the tempting trigger. I call this a pre-mortem. It can also be helpful to surround oneself with supportive individuals with similar values and goals. Additionally, seeking positive role models who have successfully navigated similar situations can provide inspiration and guidance.

Ultimately, the decision to say "no" is a keystone habit that can have a ripple effect on an individual's life. It requires discipline, courage, and a commitment to one's values and goals. By refusing to give in to peer pressure, an individual can pave the way for success and make positive decisions that align with their vision for the future. By framing this choice as an act of self-control and courage, we create an environment that encourages assertiveness and self-respect.

Keystone Decision: What Environment Should I Choose?
Choosing your environment is a keystone decision that can either set you up for success or create huge obstacles to

overcome, as it can impact many other decisions and habits. While some people may not have the opportunity to choose their living environment due to socioeconomic factors or other constraints. Those who do have a choice, deciding to live in an environment with positive influences, such as a supportive community and access to healthy lifestyle options, can significantly increase their chances of making positive lifestyle choices. In addition, such an environment can encourage an individual to decide to engage in positive habits such as regular exercise, healthy eating, and socializing with positive peers.

On the other hand, if someone chooses to live in an environment with negative influences, such as a community with high rates of drug use or crime, they may be more likely to decide to engage in negative habits such as drug use, criminal behavior, or a sedentary lifestyle.

An example of how an environment can impact behavior can be seen in a study on soldiers returning from the Vietnam War who were heroin users, commonly known as the "Vietnam War Era Study."[46] It was conducted by the U.S. government in the early 1970s. It followed over 1,600 soldiers who had been addicted to heroin while serving in Vietnam and tracked their behavior after they returned to the United States. The study found that soldiers who returned to an environment where heroin was readily available were much more likely to relapse and continue using heroin than soldiers who returned to an environment where heroin was not as easily accessible. This suggests that environmental factors played a significant role in the soldiers' decision whether to continue to use drugs or not and highlights

---

[46] Robins, L. N., Davis, D. H., & Nurco, D. N. (1974). How permanent was Vietnam drug addiction? American Journal of Public Health, 64(12 Suppl), 38–43.

the importance of creating a supportive and drug-free environment for those struggling with addiction.

Proactively choosing your environment is, therefore, an important keystone decision. By consciously selecting a positive and supportive environment, our default decision is to choose those options within this environment rather than traveling to other environments.

Keystone Decision: What Social Circle Should I Choose?

Choosing the right friends to associate with is similar to choosing the right environment. If someone surrounds themself with positive, supportive, and motivated individuals, they are more likely to engage in behaviors that align with those values. On the other hand, if someone associates with negative or unhealthy individuals, they may be more likely to engage in negative behaviors. By carefully selecting our social circle, we set ourselves up for success through *positive reinforcement* and *accountability*.

The saying "You are the average of the five people you spend the most time with" is often attributed to motivational speaker Jim Rohn. The idea behind the saying is that the people we surround ourselves with have a significant influence on our attitudes, behaviors, and overall success in life. If we surround ourselves with positive, successful, and driven individuals, we are more likely to make decisions that will lead us to adopt similar qualities and achieve our goals. On the other hand, if we associate with negative, unmotivated, or toxic people, we may find ourselves making the same decisions they have and ending up with similar attitudes and behaviors, which can hold us back and prevent us from achieving our full potential.

Keystone Decision: Where to Spend Your Time and Energy

Deciding where we spend our time and energy is the most important keystone decision of all. Time and energy are two of our most precious resources, and where we choose to direct them can significantly impact our lives. Moreover, how we spend our time and energy determines the paths we take, the relationships we form, and the achievements we make.

Choosing where to spend our time and energy requires careful consideration and intentionality. First, we should ask ourselves what is truly important in life, career, and business so that we may prioritize our goals and the actions we need to take to achieve them. We would then spend it on those areas where we get the highest return on these two precious resources. By aligning our time and energy with our values and goals, we can set ourselves up for success and fulfillment.

It is important to recognize that time and energy are finite resources and must use them wisely. This means saying no to activities, relationships, and commitments that do not serve us or align with our values and goals. It can be difficult to let go of certain things, but doing so allows us to focus our time and energy on the things that truly matter.

Ultimately, where we choose to spend our time and energy determines everything. It shapes our experiences, our relationships, and our sense of purpose. We can live more fulfilling and meaningful lives by making intentional choices and aligning our time and energy with our values and goals. By consciously choosing activities and pursuits that align with our values and goals, we create a *default* framework that guides our actions and priorities.

How to Identify and Prioritize Keystone Decisions

Here are some steps you can take to identify and prioritize your keystone decisions:

1. Define your Goals

Start by identifying your long-term goals and what you want to achieve in different areas of your life, such as your career, relationships, health, or personal development.

2. Identify Potential Keystone Decisions

Consider the decisions that have the potential to create a domino effect of positive outcomes in different areas of your life. These decisions could be related to habits, routines, relationships, or other factors that significantly impact your life.

3. Evaluate the Impact

Assess the potential impact of each keystone decision on your life, career, or business and determine which ones are most likely to set you up for success. Consider the short-term and long-term consequences of each decision and how they align with your values and goals.

4. Prioritize your Decisions

Once you have identified potential keystone decisions and evaluated their impact, prioritize them based on their level of importance and potential impact on your life. Next, determine which decisions you need to make first and which ones can wait.

5. Implement your Decisions

Once you have identified and prioritized your keystone decisions, take action to implement them into your life. Be mindful and intentional in your decision-making and make deliberate choices that align with your goals and values.

6. Consider Choice Architecture Techniques

As you identify potential keystone decisions, think about how you can apply techniques such as defaults, framing, feedback, and incentives to maximize the positive impact of these decisions.

Conclusion

Making strategic keystone decisions that have positive downstream effects on other decisions is crucial to living a fulfilling and successful life. By following a process for identifying and prioritizing keystone decisions, we can create a path to achieve our most fulfilling goals. This involves defining our goals, evaluating their impact, identifying potential keystone decisions, and prioritizing them based on their level of importance. Considering choice architecture techniques, such as defaults, framing, feedback, and incentives, is an important complement to the process. By implementing these carefully chosen keystone decisions into our lives, we can be mindful and intentional in our decision-making. This approach helps us to consider the potential consequences of our choices and make deliberate decisions based on our values and long-term goals. As a result, we can align our time and energy with our goals and values and surround ourselves with a supportive network that can help us overcome challenges and achieve our aspirations. Ultimately, making keystone decisions that leverage choice architecture techniques and set us up for success is crucial to a fulfilling life, joyful career, and thriving business.

Summary

1. Recognizing the significance of keystone decisions and making informed and strategic choices is crucial to achieving success in various aspects of our lives, as these decisions significantly impact the outcome.

2. Focusing on keystone decisions helps individuals and teams use their time and resources more efficiently.

3. Making strategic decisions with positive downstream effects can set us up for success in all areas of our lives.

4. Considering choice architecture techniques such as defaults, framing, feedback, and incentives is an important complement to the keystone decision process.

5. Choosing our environment, social circle, and where to spend our time and energy are keystone decisions that can shape our behavior and determine our success.

6. Saying no to negative habits and peer pressure is an act of courage that can prevent us from engaging in negative behaviors.

7. Mindfulness and intentional decision-making are essential to making keystone decisions that set us up for success.

8. Keystone decisions can lead to a cascade of positive outcomes in other areas of our lives.

9. Maximizing impact with strategic decisions can create a domino effect.

10. Keystone decisions can help streamline the decision-making process and ensure we direct efforts toward the most crucial choices.

Questions

1. What are keystone decisions?

   Critical decisions that lead to a cascade of outcomes in other areas.

2. How can making keystone decisions set us up for success?

   We can create a domino effect that maximizes our impact.

3. What are some examples of keystone decisions?

   Changing email addresses, setting a consistent bedtime, planning meals and grocery shopping in advance.

   What is Choice Architecture?

   The design and presentation of choices to influence decision-making while preserving freedom of choice.

4. What is the key to making keystone decisions that set us up for success?

   Mindfulness and intentional decision-making.

5. What are some key factors to consider when identifying a keystone decision?

   It should be both high-impact and high-leverage.

6. How can we cultivate the habit of making keystone decisions?

   Set aside dedicated time to reflect on your goals and identify the decisions that will have the most impact on achieving them.

7. How can keystone decisions help us avoid decision fatigue?

   We can avoid getting bogged down by other decisions.

8. How can we measure the impact of keystone decisions?

   One way is to track the outcomes of related decisions over time.

9. How can keystone decisions benefit teams and organizations?

   They can help align efforts and resources toward the most impactful decisions and build a shared sense of purpose.

Exercises

1. Change your email address and see how much free time and energy you gain.
2. Create a consistent bedtime routine to improve your sleep quality.
3. Plan your meals and grocery shopping in advance to save time and eat healthier.
4. Set a daily or weekly exercise goal to improve your physical and mental health.
5. Identify negative influences in your social circle and make a conscious effort to distance yourself from them.
6. Create a budget and track your expenses to better manage your finances.
7. Identify and eliminate unnecessary commitments and obligations to free up your time.
8. Practice mindfulness and intentional decision-making to make more effective choices.
9. Prioritize your most important goals and identify the keystone decisions to help you achieve them.
10. Identify other keystone decisions that can save you time and energy by reducing downstream decisions.

Principle 12

Defeat Analysis Paralysis, Decision Fatigue, and Indecision

"In any moment of decision, the best thing you can do is the right thing, the next best thing is the wrong thing, and the worst thing you can do is nothing."

—*Theodore Roosevelt*

Unleashing the Power of Decisiveness in a Fast-Paced World

Overcoming analysis paralysis, decision fatigue, and indecision involves making decisions and taking action in a timely manner rather than becoming overwhelmed by the decision-making process. By being decisive and taking calculated risks, individuals and teams can move forward and achieve their goals, ensuring that opportunities are not missed in a rapidly changing world.

Key Question

How can we utilize proven strategies to overcome analysis paralysis, decision fatigue, and information overload in order to unleash the power of decisiveness in a fast-paced world?

This chapter explores the challenges of analysis paralysis, decision fatigue, and information overload and the resulting indecision that many individuals and businesses face in today's fast-paced world. Through the lens of proven strategies and techniques, the chapter provides guidance on how to unleash the power of decisiveness to achieve success in the personal, professional, and business realms. The chapter covers topics such as the criteria for deciding the degree of analysis required, the differences between System 1 and System 2 decisions, the dangers of information overload, decision fatigue, high-velocity decision-making, and techniques for overcoming analysis paralysis and indecision.

In a world where information is readily available, and decisions need to be made quickly, analysis paralysis and indecision can be overwhelming. The ability to make both efficient and effective decisions is a critical skill for success in both personal and professional domains. When individuals are unable to make decisions or become stuck in analysis paralysis, it can lead to missed opportunities, reduced productivity, and increased stress. This chapter is important because it provides practical strategies and techniques for overcoming analysis paralysis and decision fatigue, making effective decisions, and developing decisiveness as a valuable skill. By embracing proven strategies, individuals can avoid these pitfalls in order to make confident, efficient, and bold decisions that lead to success.

What Is Analysis Paralysis?

Analysis paralysis refers to a situation where an individual or a group becomes so overwhelmed by the available options and the complexity of a decision that they become unable to make a choice. In other words, analysis paralysis occurs when a person becomes stuck in the analysis phase of decision-making, unable to move forward with a decision due to a perceived need for more information, analysis, or certainty. This can happen in any arena. For example, research by psychologists Sheena Iyengar and Mark Lepper found that, when presented with a selection of 24 different jams, consumers were more likely to purchase when only presented with six options. This demonstrates that having too many choices can lead to indecision and a lack of action.[47] This can be a frustrating and unproductive state to be in, as it can lead to missed opportunities, wasted time and

---

[47] Roger Martin, "More Isn't Always Better," Harvard Business Review, June 1, 2006, https://hbr.org/2006/06/more-isnt-always-better.

resources, and increased stress and anxiety. Analysis paralysis can also cause decision-makers to lose confidence in their abilities, leading to a further delay in making a decision.

The Pitfalls of Analysis Paralysis

Analysis paralysis can be a major obstacle to progress, as individuals can become so consumed with weighing all the possible options that they fail to act. This challenge can be particularly daunting in a fast-paced world where decisions must be made quickly and decisively. Moreover, the inability to make decisions can lead to missed opportunities, as the window for action may close before a choice can be made. This can be particularly true in competitive industries where opportunities are often fleeting, and the ability to seize them can be the difference between success and failure.

Moreover, analysis paralysis can lead to reduced productivity as individuals become bogged down by indecision. This can be especially problematic in business settings where time is money, and the ability to make quick, effective decisions can be critical to success. In addition to lost opportunities and reduced productivity, analysis paralysis can lead to increased stress and anxiety. When individuals are unable to make decisions, they may worry about the potential consequences of their inaction, which can lead to feelings of overwhelm and helplessness. Ultimately, overcoming analysis paralysis and developing the skill of decisiveness can be crucial to achieving success in both personal and professional endeavors.

Degree of Analysis Required: The Criteria

Miscalculating the degree of analysis required for a given decision is the key factor among those who tend to get stuck in this insidious trap. For the most part, the amount of analysis required for a decision depends on two things. The "deadline" for the decision and the "impact" that the decision will have. Below is a more complete list to consider when deciding the degree of analysis necessary for a given decision:

1. Time Sensitivity

Decisions that need to be made quickly may not allow for extensive analysis. In these cases, decision-makers might rely more on intuition and previous experiences. For example, decisions must be made rapidly during an emergency to address the urgent situation.

2. Impact

The potential consequences of a decision can influence the depth of analysis required. High-impact decisions, such as strategic business moves or significant personal choices, warrant a more thorough analysis to minimize potential risks and ensure positive outcomes. In contrast, low-impact decisions, such as choosing a meal at a restaurant, may require less analysis.

3. Complexity

The more complex a decision is, the more analysis it may require. This is because complex decisions often involve multiple factors, stakeholders, and possible outcomes. For example, selecting a new software system for a company may require an in-depth analysis of features, costs, and compatibility with existing systems.

4. Uncertainty

Decisions that involve a high degree of uncertainty may require more analysis to reduce risks and make more informed choices. For instance, investing in a start-up business can be uncertain due to the lack of historical data and lack of proven business models and will require investors to conduct thorough research and carefully assess potential risks and rewards.

5. Availability of Information

The amount and quality of available information can influence the degree of analysis needed. Decision can conduct a more comprehensive analysis with ample, reliable information. Conversely, limited or low-quality information may hinder in-depth analysis and require decision-makers to rely more on intuition or other sources of information.

6. Stakeholder Involvement

Decisions that involve multiple stakeholders may require a higher degree of analysis to address the diverse interests, opinions, and perspectives. For example, implementing a new company policy may require gathering input from various departments and considering the potential impact on different employees.

Reversible vs. Irreversible Decisions that Impact Analysis

The concept of Type 1 (T1) and Type 2 (T2) decisions was popularized by Jeff Bezos, the founder of Amazon, in his 2016 letter to Amazon shareholders.[48] According to Bezos, these two types of decisions are distinguished by their level of impact, reversibility, and the decision-making approach they require.

Type 1 (T1) decisions are high-impact, consequential decisions that are difficult to reverse or undo. They require thorough analysis, planning, and evaluation because the potential risks and outcomes are significant. In addition, these decisions often have long-term implications and can significantly impact the organization or individual making the decision.

Type 2 (T2) decisions, on the other hand, are lower-impact decisions that can be easily reversed or adjusted if the initial choice proves to be suboptimal. Bezos argues that these decisions should be made more quickly and with less extensive analysis because they pose less risk and can be easily changed if necessary.

Bezos emphasizes the importance of recognizing the difference between these two types of decisions and adapting the decision-making process accordingly. He believes that many

---

[48] Bezos, J. (2016). 2016 Letter to Amazon Shareholders. Amazon.com, Inc. Retrieved from https://www.aboutamazon.com/news/company-news/2016-letter-to-shareholders

organizations spend too much time deliberating over Type 2 decisions, which slows down innovation and progress.

So, after reaching a degree of research and analysis that aligns with the importance of the decision, it's imperative to commit to your chosen path. Doubting your decisions or constantly revisiting them can lead to lost opportunities and reduced efficiency. Decisiveness is vital in turning your choices into successful outcomes.

Decision Fatigue

What is it? Decision fatigue is a phenomenon that occurs when individuals experience a decline in decision-making quality and self-control after making a series of decisions. It is a mental state that arises when people are confronted with a large number of choices, resulting in decision-making fatigue.

Fast fact: According to Asana's most recent Anatomy of Work Special Report, seven in ten executives say that burnout has affected their decision-making abilities.[49] This can lead to suboptimal decisions, such as impulsive purchases, irrational choices, or a lack of decision-making altogether.

Decision fatigue is a significant issue in today's fast-paced society, where individuals are constantly faced with choices and decisions. It can occur in many different contexts, including personal life, work, and other areas where individuals are required to make decisions. Decision fatigue can lead to missed opportunities, reduced productivity, and negative health

---

[49] Asana. (2022). *Anatomy of Work Global Index 2022.*
https://investors.asana.com/news/news-details/2022/Asana-Anatomy-of-Work-Index-2022-Work-About-Work-Hampering-Organizational-Agility/default.aspx

outcomes. For instance, decision fatigue can lead to a decrease in self-control, causing individuals to eat unhealthy foods or engage in other unhealthy behaviors.

Why Does Decision Fatigue Occur?

Decision fatigue can occur in a variety of ways. One of the primary causes is the sheer number of decisions that people are faced with on a daily basis. The more decisions that must be made, the more mental energy is required, leading to decision-making fatigue. Additionally, the complexity of decisions can contribute to decision fatigue. Difficult decisions, those with high stakes, or those requiring a lot of analysis can lead to a decrease in mental energy and focus. Persistent decision fatigue can even affect your health. A study in *The Journal of Clinical Nursing* found that decision fatigue can even negatively affect the quality that healthcare patients receive, as it can impair nurses' ability to make sound clinical choices about patient care.[50] Another factor that can contribute to decision fatigue is the timing of decisions. Research has shown that individuals are more likely to experience decision fatigue later in the day after making a large number of decisions. This is because decision-making requires mental energy, which can be depleted over time. As a result, people tend to make poorer decisions in the late afternoon and evening than they do earlier in the day.

Mitigating and Eliminating Decision Fatigue

To mitigate decision fatigue, there are several strategies that individuals can employ.

1. Limit Decisions

One of the most effective strategies is to *limit the number of decisions* that need to be made. For example, as discussed in the previous chapter, you could change your email address, thereby reducing the number of emails and the corresponding decisions that need to be made for each of them. Or, like Steve Jobs, you

---

[50] Pignatiello, G. A., Tsivitse, E., O'Brien, J., Kraus, N., & Hickman, R. L., Jr (2022). Decision fatigue among clinical nurses during the COVID-19 pandemic. *Journal of clinical nursing*, 31*(7-8)*, 869–877.

could decide to wear the same outfit each day! Another strategy is to break up complex decisions into smaller, more manageable parts. This allows individuals to focus on one aspect of the decision at a time, reducing the overall mental energy required.

2. Make Decisions Early in the Day

Another approach is to *make important decisions earlier in the day* when mental energy is higher. This can help to ensure that important decisions are made with a clear mind and that individuals are less likely to experience decision fatigue.

3. Practice Self Care

Finally, individuals can *practice self-care strategies*, such as getting enough sleep, eating a healthy diet, and exercising regularly. These strategies can help ensure they have the mental and physical energy required to make good decisions.

Decision fatigue is a significant issue that can impact individuals' productivity, health, and overall quality of life. It can occur due to the number and complexity of decisions required, as well as the timing of decisions. However, there are several strategies that individuals can employ to mitigate or eliminate decision fatigue, including limiting the number of decisions required, breaking up complex decisions, and practicing self-care. By doing so, individuals can ensure they are making good decisions and achieving their goals.

Information Overload

What is it? **Information overload** refers to the state of being overwhelmed with too much information, to the point that it becomes difficult to process and make sense of it all. With the rise of technology and the internet, we have access to enormous amounts of information at our fingertips. This can be both a blessing and a curse. When individuals are presented with too much information, they may experience cognitive overload, leading to decision fatigue.

Information overload can contribute to decision fatigue by making it difficult for individuals to filter out the most important and relevant information needed to make a decision. When individuals are presented with an abundance of options or information, they may become overwhelmed and struggle to focus on the most important factors. This can result in decision-making becoming more difficult and time-consuming, leading to increased stress and frustration.

Moreover, constantly processing information can also be mentally taxing, causing individuals to experience decision fatigue. When individuals are presented with an excessive amount of information, they may need to devote more cognitive resources to the decision-making process, which can lead to mental exhaustion. This, in turn, can lead to poor decision-making, as individuals may become less able to make sound judgments and become more fatigued.

Overall, information overload can significantly impact on decision-making, leading to decision fatigue and reduced productivity. Therefore, it's important to learn how to effectively manage and filter information so that we can avoid becoming overwhelmed and make informed decisions without sacrificing mental clarity or well-being.

Mitigating and Eliminating Information Overload

There are several ways to overcome information overload and mitigate its impact on decision fatigue:

1. Set Clear Goals and Priorities
Start by defining your goals and identifying the information you need to make a decision. Then, prioritize the most important information and focus on obtaining that first. This will help you avoid getting bogged down by irrelevant or less important information.

2. Limit your Options

When faced with too many options, it's easy to become overwhelmed and unable to make a decision. Consider narrowing down your options by setting specific criteria or eliminating those that don't meet your needs. This can help simplify the decision-making process and reduce the amount of information you need to consider.

3. Use Technology to Your Advantage

There are many tools and applications available that can help you organize and manage information. Consider using a note-taking app, bookmarking tool, or another organizational software to keep track of relevant information and reduce the time spent searching for it.

4. Take Breaks and Practice Self-care

Decision fatigue can lead to stress, exhaustion, and burnout. Taking regular breaks, practicing mindfulness, and engaging in activities that promote relaxation and self-care can help you reduce the impact of information overload and decision fatigue.

5. Seek Input from Others

Collaborating with others and seeking input from trusted sources can help reduce the burden of decision-making and provide additional perspectives and insights. Consider consulting with colleagues, mentors, or experts in the field to help inform your decisions and reduce the impact of information overload.

By implementing these strategies, you can overcome information overload and, in turn, reduce your chances of developing decision fatigue, enabling you to make more informed and effective decisions.

High-Velocity Decision-Making

High-velocity decision-making refers to the process of making quick and effective decisions in a fast-paced and constantly changing environment. This approach to decision-making emphasizes speed, efficiency, and a willingness to take calculated risks rather than waiting for complete information or analysis. High-velocity decision-making is becoming increasingly important in today's world due to rapid technological advancements, increased competition, and a need for businesses to remain agile and adaptable.

The origin of the concept of high-velocity decision-making can, again, be traced back to Jeff Bezos. In another letter to shareholders from 2015, Bezos outlined four key principles that guide Amazon's decision-making process:

1. Speed Matters in Business

In today's fast-paced business environment, speed matters. Being able to make decisions quickly and efficiently can give companies a competitive advantage over their slower-moving counterparts. Rapid decision-making can help organizations respond to market changes, capitalize on emerging opportunities, and stay ahead of the curve. However, it's important to balance speed with accuracy and avoid hasty decisions that may lead to negative consequences. By using data-driven insights and collaborating effectively, businesses can make informed decisions in a timely manner.

2. Make Decisions with 70% of the Information You Wish You Had

When making decisions, it's easy to fall into the trap of analysis paralysis, waiting for all the information to be available before taking action. However, this can lead to missed opportunities and delayed progress. A better approach is to make decisions with around 70% of the information you wish you had. This means gathering enough information to make an informed decision but not waiting for every last piece of data. This approach allows decision makers to act quickly while making well-informed choices.

3. Disagree and Commit

As I noted in Chapter 3, disagree and commit is a leadership principle that states that when there is disagreement among team members, it's important to work through those disagreements and come to a resolution. *However*, once a decision is made by whoever is accountable for the decision, everyone must commit to it, even if they initially disagreed. This allows the team to move forward with a unified focus and avoid getting bogged down by ongoing debates or personal preferences. Disagree and commit encourages healthy debate and collaboration while also promoting decisive action. At Arootah, I always use the analogy of going into battle. If time permits, there can and should be a debate before the battle starts ... but once the battle begins, we must all be aligned with the mission and execute it as if it were our very own creation, whether we agreed with it or not during the debate period.

By the way, I always let my team know that unless we have a majorly tight deadline, they are all encouraged to and will be given a chance to make their case about any major decision. In that same vein, I bring up this hypothetical question in all my interviews. I lay out the following scenario: We have a disagreement about a major policy issue. I will give you a chance to debate it openly with the team and me. If at the end of the debate, I still disagree, and we move forward with my decision, but it turns out that I was wrong and they were right, whose fault is it? The inclination, of course, would be to say that I was wrong because I didn't agree with their position, and many give that answer. WRONG! The nice ones say it's nobody's fault! We should just all get along! They don't get the job. However, those candidates who think a little deeper about the question usually get it right. The correct answer is that, even though they were on the right side of the decision, they were still at fault because they didn't make their case strong enough during the debate. You see, there are only two reasons why I wouldn't agree with them. One illogical and one logical.

1. *I'm an egomaniac, and I just want to get my way even if I am wrong (which may indeed be the case sometimes! Who likes to be wrong! Especially in front of the whole team!). But this is an illogical reason because it is my company, so if I went around making the wrong decisions because of ego, we wouldn't do very well (not to say that many companies don't do this.)*

OR

2. *They didn't make their case in the time allotted. They weren't prepared. This is why I insist that all important decisions for Blue Ridge and Arootah go through our rigorous process. If anybody does that, the decision is usually clear. The most common question at my company when there is an important decision to be made is, "Did you put it through the Decision Manager" (our decision-making software)? If not, we don't want to waste our time debating it. Do the work and then present the recommendations.*

4. Recognize Misalignment Issues Early and Escalate them Immediately

In any organization, there will be times when team members have different goals, values, or priorities. When these misalignments occur, it's important to recognize them early and address them proactively. This can prevent conflicts from escalating and ensure everyone works toward the same goals. Escalating misalignment issues early can also help teams avoid wasted time and resources on initiatives that are unlikely to succeed. By identifying misalignments and working to resolve them, teams can achieve greater cohesion and collaboration.

Bezos believed that the traditional approach to decision-making, which involved gathering all available information, analyzing it, and deliberating at length, was too slow and inefficient in today's fast-paced business environment. He advocated for a more agile and decisive approach, where decisions are made quickly, based on incomplete information if necessary, and with a willingness to course-correct if needed.

Amazon has since become well-known for its fast-paced decision-making culture, which emphasizes experimentation, risk-taking, and a willingness to pivot quickly based on feedback and results. Other companies and organizations have also adopted high-velocity decision-making practices in order to remain competitive and agile in rapidly changing industries.

Throw a Dart?

The idea behind "If all else fails, throw a dart" is that sometimes it is better to make a decision— any decision — than get stuck in analysis paralysis and indecision. While this approach may work in some situations, it's important to note that it is not always true. Hasty or uninformed decisions can lead to negative consequences, especially in high-stakes situations. The quotation by Theodore Roosevelt at the beginning of the chapter highlights the importance of at least making a decision, which can be a decision to do nothing. However, it's important to note that making the wrong decision can also have negative consequences.

I think the more accurate point to be made here is to be sure that you recognize the other option: NO DECISION. No-Decision *is* a decision. It's a decision to do nothing. This option should always be factored into the equation as a legitimate option, but it is often neglected for some reason.

There are decisions where it does make sense to choose randomly (*i.e.*, throw a dart, pick from a hat, or flip a coin if there are only two choices). If you, for some reason just can't decide amongst the other options due to the reasons mentioned in this chapter (or other reasons) *and* you determine that the other options are all better than the NO DECISION option, then logic would have it that you do, in fact, randomly choose an option other than no decision.

This situation recently happened to me. I was informed that I had some funds in a checking account, earning ZERO interest. I was presented with two Money Market options that were very close in terms of interest rates but had some minor differences with respect to fees and tax impact, etc. I could have studied the details, made a call or two, etc., but it wasn't worth my time because I knew the difference would be tiny at the end of the day. Rather than wallow in indecision and earn zero interest for another day, I just picked one.

Here are three more hypothetical examples of this type of situation:

1. You are trying to decide between two restaurants for dinner, but you can't decide based on online reviews and recommendations. However, you know both restaurants are better than staying home and eating leftovers. In this case, throwing a dart or flipping a coin could be a reasonable approach to deciding.

2. You are trying to choose between two job offers but can't decide based on salary, benefits, and company culture. However, you know that both jobs are better than staying unemployed. In this case, throwing a dart or flipping a coin could help you decide and move forward with your career.

3. You are trying to choose between two vacation destinations but can't decide based on online research and recommendations. However, you know both destinations are better than staying home and not taking a vacation. In this case, throwing a dart or flipping a coin could help you choose a destination and enjoy a much-needed break.

A final point here that I recently heard on a podcast was that if it's a close call, it's reversible, and the downside isn't terrible. The benefits of making a faster decision, even with less information, are that if you're wrong, at least you will find out sooner, enabling you to course-correct faster!

In summary, while "If all else fails, throw a dart" can be a good strategy to utilize in some relatively low-stakes situations, it's not always true. The best approach depends on the context and the level of impact and reversibility of the decision. The key is to strike a balance between analysis and action while making a decision that is informed, timely, and aligned with one's goals and values.

Conclusion

Making decisions quickly and confidently is a critical skill in today's fast-paced world. Analysis paralysis, decision fatigue, and information overload can all lead to indecision. Indecision or slow decisions usually result in missed opportunities, reduced productivity, and increased stress. This chapter provides practical strategies and techniques for overcoming these obstacles. By embracing these proven strategies, individuals can avoid these insidious pitfalls and learn to make efficient and effective decisions that lead to success. As Theodore Roosevelt said, "The best thing you can do is the right thing, the next best thing is the wrong thing, and the worst thing you can do is nothing." Therefore, individuals must learn to confidently make decisions and avoid analysis paralysis and decision fatigue.

Summary

1. Overcoming analysis paralysis, decision fatigue, and indecision is essential for effective decision-making.
2. Analysis paralysis occurs when an individual becomes stuck in the analysis phase of decision-making, unable to move forward with a decision.
3. High-impact decisions require a more thorough analysis to minimize potential risks and ensure positive outcomes.
4. Decision fatigue is a mental state that arises when individuals experience a decline in decision-making quality and self-control after making a series of decisions.
5. To mitigate decision fatigue, individuals can limit decisions, make decisions early in the day, and practice self-care.
6. Information overload can lead to decision fatigue, but individuals can overcome it by setting clear goals, prioritizing information, and using technology to their advantage.
7. High-velocity decision-making emphasizes speed, efficiency, and a willingness to take calculated risks.
8. When making decisions, individuals should aim to gather around 70% of the information they wish they had.
9. Disagree and commit is a strategy that encourages individuals to support a decision even if they disagree with it.
10. Making decisions with confidence and avoiding analysis paralysis and decision fatigue are critical skills in today's fast-paced world.

Questions

1. What is analysis paralysis?

   Where you become overwhelmed and unable to decide.

2. What are the pitfalls of analysis paralysis?

   Becoming so consumed that they fail to act.

3. What is decision fatigue?

   When one losses energy facing a large number of choices.

4. How does decision fatigue occur?

   By the number of decisions that you face on a daily basis, the complexity of decisions, or those requiring a lot of analysis.

5. What are some strategies to mitigate decision fatigue?

   Limiting the number of decisions that need to be made and making important decisions earlier in the day when mental energy is higher.

6. What is information overload?

   The state of being overwhelmed with too much information, to the point where it becomes difficult to process and make sense of it all.

7. How can individuals mitigate and eliminate information overload?

   By setting clear goals and priorities and limiting options

8. What is high-velocity decision-making?

   The process of making quick and effective decisions in a fast-paced and constantly changing environment.

9. What is the disagree and commit approach to decision-making?

   It encourages individuals to voice their opinions and concerns while still committing to the ultimate decision made by the team or organization.

10. What is the "throw a dart" approach to decision-making?

    It suggests that sometimes it is better to make a decision (any decision) than to get stuck in analysis paralysis and indecision.

Exercises

1. Make a list of three decisions you've been putting off due to analysis paralysis. Then, identify the criteria for analyzing these decisions and determine a deadline for making a decision.

2. Keep track of the number of decisions you make in a day. At the end of the day, reflect on whether you experienced decision fatigue and identify any strategies that helped mitigate it.

3. Choose a high-impact decision you need to make, such as whether to switch careers. Then, identify the information you need to make the decision and prioritize it based on its importance.

4. Find an article or research study on analysis paralysis or decision fatigue and summarize the main findings.

5. Write down a list of the different sources of information you rely on to make decisions. Then, identify any sources that may contribute to information overload and consider how you can limit their impact.

6. Choose a decision you need to make quick, such as whether to accept a job offer. Reflect on the strategies you can use to make a quick and effective decision.

7. Identify a recent decision you made where you waited too long for additional information. Consider how you could have made the decision with around 70% of the information you wish you had.

8. Choose a decision you made where you initially disagreed but eventually committed to the decision. Reflect on how this strategy could be used in other areas of your life.

9. Find a TED Talk or podcast on decision-making and take notes on the speaker's key points and strategies for making effective decisions.

10. Reflect on a past decision where you experienced analysis paralysis or decision fatigue. Identify any strategies you can use in the future to avoid these pitfalls.

Conclusion

In conclusion, effective decision-making is an essential skill for leaders in all aspects of life. Whether in personal or professional settings, leaders face complex and challenging decision-making scenarios every day. The ability to navigate these challenges and make informed choices can be the difference between success and failure and, ultimately, whether we live fulfilling life.

We have presented 12 key Principles in this book, designed to help leaders conquer common decision-making obstacles. By mastering the art and science of decision-making with these Principles, leaders can develop a more robust decision-making process and achieve more fulfilling outcomes. These principles cover a range of decision-making challenges that can be conquered. By applying these principles, leaders can navigate complex decision-making scenarios and achieve greater success and fulfillment in their personal and professional lives.

However, we recognize that knowledge does not apply itself. To truly master these principles, it is important to engage in exercises and practical applications. That's why we have included exercises at the end of each chapter to help readers apply the principles to their own decision-making scenarios. The best way to learn is heuristically. We also encourage readers to take the time to reflect on the key questions posed in each chapter, engage in the exercises, and apply the principles to their own decision-making scenarios. By doing so, we believe they will be better equipped to navigate complex decision-making scenarios and achieve greater success in life, career, and business.

About Arootah

Arootah is a coaching and advisory business serving financial services executives who want to unlock potential in their companies and lives. We devise pragmatic strategies that stimulate growth, inspire peak performance, and strengthen accountability. We've identified and distilled proven behaviors at the intersection of finance, technology, and wellness. Our clients are empowered to raise their standards, overcome their challenges, and achieve results.

AROOTAH

Resources

Decision Manager App

Leverage technology with a tool that provides a process to analyze your options, ensuring that any major decision you're facing is made with confidence.

- Eliminate biases that cloud judgment
- Develop conviction in your decisiveness
- Make informed choices to achieve better outcomes

Learn More: https://arootah.com/apps/

Habit Accountability Tracker App

The Arootah Habit Accountability Tracker App keeps you on track toward living the life you most desire. Enjoy the compounding effect of small daily wins that result in a lifetime of positive transformation.

Learn More: https://arootah.com/apps/

Software and Apps

Arootah Software and Apps allow you to leverage technology to optimize your most precious resource: time. Our apps help you gain clarity in chaos, improve your judgment in decision-making, and accomplish the goals to elevate your life.

Learn More: https://arootah.com/apps/

Speaking Engagements

Arootah Speaking Engagements offers actionable leadership, work culture, goal setting, and energy optimization to motivate teams to achieve greater success. Whether your team wants to earn more business, accomplish work/life goals, or adopt healthier habits, we provide the roadmap.

Learn More: https://arootah.com/about/speaking-engagements/

Executive Coaching

Arootah Executive Coaching gives corporate leaders and other financial executives an edge by infusing technology into coaching to elevate clarity, strategy, and accountability. Our coaches can empower you to harness opportunities, overcome institutional challenges, and lead with a roadmap.

Learn More: https://arootah.com/executive-coaching/

Leadership Training

Arootah Leadership Training is designed by executives for executives as drawn from Rich Bello's impactful career. Learn to maximize your influence and create a positive ripple effect throughout the organization.

Peak Performance topics include, but are not limited to:

- Mindset
- Time Management
- Decision-making
- Goal Setting
- Energy, Discipline, & Focus
- Procrastination

Learn More: https://arootah.com/leadership-development-trainings/

Team Coaching

To transform your business, invest in your people. Arootah Team Coaching helps teams discover their most innovative strategies for working together propel the firm forward. Teams will leave with heightened collaboration and decision-making skills, self-leadership, and collective productivity.

Learn More: https://arootah.com/team-coaching/

Business Consulting

Arootah Business Consulting advises hedge fund executives, single-family offices, and multi-family offices on how to maximize performance across Investments and Operations, leveraging the expertise of advisors from some of the world's most prestigious firms.

Learn More: https://arootah.com/business-consulting/

Hedge Fund Advisory

Arootah Hedge Fund Advisory propels your business forward by leveraging our experience across the key areas of a firm: investments and operations. Our industry veterans will support you throughout the entire life cycle: from startup to raising capital to ongoing operations and beyond.

Learn More: https://arootah.com/business-consulting/hedge-fund/

Family Office Advisory

Arootah Family Office Advisory supports the unsung heroes who drive the engine of all aspects of a family office, including philanthropy, business ventures, wealth preservation, and more. Our experience managing family offices helps your clients navigate the three most valuable assets: time, money, and family.

Learn More: https://arootah.com/business-consulting/family-offices/

Remote Work Advisory

Arootah Remote Work Advisory offers strategies to leverage global opportunities and manage resources. We've led through the most unforeseen events of the last 25 years, minimizing disruption and maximizing opportunity.

Learn More: https://arootah.com/remote-work-advisory/

Corporate Wellness

Arootah Corporate Wellness is a comprehensive well-being solution that brings greater productivity, improves employee engagement, and strengthens workplace culture. Our comprehensive program leverages health coaching, nutrition, fitness, and stress management from a Chief Wellness Officer.

Learn More: https://arootah.com/corporate-wellness/

Talent Acquisition

From attracting top talent to creating fair, consistent recruiting processes, Arootah Talent Acquisition services support HR leaders to thrive at every stage of the employee lifecycle.

Learn More: https://arootah.com/talent-acquisition/

Health Coaching

Arootah Health Coaching supports wellness that combines expertise in overall well-being with accountability strategies to keep you on track. Leverage technology to create impactful habits and control over your energy.

Learn More: https://arootah.com/personal/health-coaching/

Life Coaching

Arootah Life Coaching supports you in creating a life aligned with your highest priorities. We enhance coaching with technology while our coaches motivate you to bridge the gap between where you are and where you want to be, to lead a life that supports what matters most to you.

Learn More: https://arootah.com/personal/life-coaching/

Career Coaching

Arootah Career Coaching illuminates the career that will link your talents to your desired professional trajectory. We can help you navigate transitions, explore new career paths, and advance in your industry.

Learn More: https://arootah.com/career-coaching/

Remote Work Coaching

Arootah Remote Work Coaching infuses technology in coaching to combat proximity bias. Empowering you to lead your business with frictionless progress, autonomy, and liberation.

Learn More: https://arootah.com/remote-work-coaching/

Appendix I

By prioritizing and weighing the criteria, you can ensure that your decision is based on a balanced and well-informed assessment of all relevant factors. Each process helps to minimize the impact of subjective biases and ensures that your decision aligns with your priorities and objectives. We will continue with the example of purchasing a home to prioritize and weigh the criteria under each method.

1. List Comparison Method - Example

Let's continue with the example of purchasing a home in a suburban neighborhood. We previously *identified* the top ten criteria. Below is the ***initial list*** of criteria:

1. Affordability
2. School district quality
3. Commute time
4. Neighborhood safety
5. Proximity to amenities
6. Nice kitchen
7. Large backyard
8. Number of bedrooms
9. Number of bathrooms
10. Home's overall condition

Part 1: Prioritizing the Criteria

Using the list comparison iterative processes described previously, we arrive at a ***prioritized list*** of the criteria as follows:

1. Affordability
2. School district quality
3. Neighborhood safety
4. Commute time
5. Proximity to amenities
6. Number of bedrooms

7. Number of bathrooms
8. Nice kitchen
9. Large backyard
10. Home's overall condition

Part 2: Assigning Weights to the Criteria
There are various methods you can apply to this process. All are more or less subjective judgment based.

Linear Method (described previously):

1. Affordability: 10
2. School district quality: 9
3. Neighborhood safety: 8
4. Commute time: 7
5. Proximity to amenities: 6
6. Number of bedrooms: 5
7. Number of bathrooms: 4
8. Nice kitchen: 3
9. Large backyard: 2
10. Home's overall condition: 1

Now we'll normalize the weights so that they sum up to 100%. To do this, we can sum the assigned values (10+9+8+7+6+5+4+3+2+1=55) and divide each value by the total sum:

1. Affordability: 10/55 = (18.18%)
2. School district quality: 9/55 = (16.36%)
3. Neighborhood safety: 8/55 = (14.55%)
4. Commute time: 7/55 = (12.73%)
5. Proximity to amenities: 6/55 = (10.91%)
6. Number of bedrooms: 5/55 = (9.09%)
7. Number of bathrooms: 4/55 = (7.27%)
8. Nice kitchen: 3/55 = (5.45%)
9. Large backyard: 2/55 = (3.64%)
10. Home's overall condition: 1/55 = (1.82%)

Exponential Scale Method (described previously)

Using an exponential scale to emphasize the importance of the highest priority criteria, we can assign weights as follows (using a base of 2 for simplicity):

1. Affordability: $2^9 = 512$
2. School district quality: $2^8 = 256$
3. Neighborhood safety: $2^7 = 128$
4. Commute time: $2^6 = 64$
5. Proximity to amenities: $2^5 = 32$
6. Number of bedrooms: $2^4 = 16$
7. Number of bathrooms: $2^3 = 8$
8. Nice kitchen: $2^2 = 4$
9. Large backyard: $2^1 = 2$
10. Home's overall condition: $2^0 = 1$

Now, let's normalize the weights so that they sum up to 100%. To do this, we can sum the assigned values ($512+256+128+64+32+16+8+4+2+1=1023$) and divide each value by the total sum:

1. Affordability: $512/1023 = (50.05\%)$
2. School district quality: $256/1023 = (25.02\%)$
3. Neighborhood safety: $128/1023 = (12.51\%)$
4. Commute time: $64/1023 = (6.26\%)$
5. Proximity to amenities: $32/1023 = (3.13\%)$
6. Number of bedrooms: $16/1023 = (1.56\%)$
7. Number of bathrooms: $8/1023 = (0.78\%)$
8. Nice kitchen: $4/1023 = (0.39\%)$
9. Large backyard: $2/1023 = (0.20\%)$
10. Home's overall condition: $1/1023 = (0.10\%)$

As you can see, this method results in weighting that is heavily skewed towards the highest weighted criteria rendering the lower weighted criteria practically meaningless for the decision. It would in essence be a tie breaker if all else were equal.

Lowering the base evens things out somewhat.

Using an exponential scale with a *base of 1.25* will still emphasize the importance of the highest priority criteria, but not quite as much as we will see. Let's, assign weights as follows:

1. Affordability: $1.25^9 = 7.4506$
2. School district quality: $1.25^8 = 5.9605$
3. Neighborhood safety: $1.25^7 = 4.7684$
4. Commute time: $1.25^6 = 3.8147$
5. Proximity to amenities: $1.25^5 = 3.0518$
6. Number of bedrooms: $1.25^4 = 2.4414$
7. Number of bathrooms: $1.25^3 = 1.9531$
8. Nice kitchen: $1.25^2 = 1.5625$
9. Large backyard: $1.25^1 = 1.2500$
10. Home's overall condition: $1.25^0 = 1.0000$

Now, let's normalize the weights so that they sum up to 100%. To do this, we can sum the assigned values (7.4506 + 5.9605 + 4.7684 + 3.8147 + 3.0518 + 2.4414 + 1.9531 + 1.5625 + 1.2500 + 1.0000 = 33.252) and divide each value by the total sum:

1. Affordability: 7.4506/33.252 ≈ (22.40%)
2. School district quality: 5.9605/33.252 ≈ (17.93%)
3. Neighborhood safety: 4.7684/33.252 ≈ (14.34%)
4. Commute time: 3.8147/33.252 ≈ (11.47%)
5. Proximity to amenities: 3.0518/33.252 ≈ (9.18%)
6. Number of bedrooms: 2.4414/33.252 ≈ (7.34%)
7. Number of bathrooms: 1.9531/33.252 ≈ (5.87%)
8. Nice kitchen: 1.5625/33.252 ≈ (4.70%)
9. Large backyard: 1.2500/33.252 ≈ (3.76%)
10. Home's overall condition: 1.0000/33.252 ≈ (3.01%)

Using a base of 1.25 for the exponential function results in a more evenly distributed set of weights, with less emphasis on the top criteria and more weight on the lower-ranked criteria compared to a base of 1.5 or 2.

A logarithmic approach will yield substantially the same results.

2. Pairwise Comparison Method

Let's continue with the example of purchasing a home in a suburban neighborhood. We previously *identified* the top ten criteria. Below is the ***initial list*** of criteria:

1. Price
2. School
3. Safety
4. Commute
5. Amenities
6. Bedrooms
7. Bathrooms
8. Kitchen
9. Backyard
10. Condition

Criteria		Price	School	Safety	Commute	Amenities	Bedrooms	Bathrooms	Kitchen	Backyard	Condition	Sum	Pairwise %	Pairwise Rank
1	Price	1	8	6	8	8	6	7	6	6	1	57.00	23.6%	1
2	School	1/8	1	1/8	5	7	1/2	1/2	1/2	1/2	1/9	15.36	6.4%	5
3	Safety	1/6	8	1	9	9	5	6	6	7	1	52.17	21.6%	3
4	Commute	1/8	1/5	1/9	1	1/4	1/4	1/3	1/4	1/2	1/8	3.14	1.3%	10
5	Amenities	1/8	1/7	1/9	4	1	1/3	1/2	1/2	1/2	1/9	7.32	3.0%	9
6	Bedrooms	1/6	2	1/5	4	3	1	2	3	2	1/7	17.51	7.3%	4
7	Bathrooms	1/7	2	1/6	3	2	1/2	1	1	2	1/7	11.95	5.0%	7
8	Kitchen	1/6	2	1/6	4	2	1/3	1	1	2	1/5	12.87	5.3%	6
9	Backyard	1/6	2	1/7	2	2	1/2	1/2	1/2	1	1/7	8.95	3.7%	8
10	Condition	1	9	1	8	9	7	7	5	7	1	55.00	22.8%	2
	Sum	3 1/5	34 1/3	9	48	43 1/4	21 3/7	25 5/6	23 3/4	28 1/2	4	241.28	100%	

To use the pairwise comparison method of decision-making, let's first create a matrix comparing each criterion to every other criterion. We will compare each item to each other using a scale of 1 to 10, where 1 indicates equal importance, and 10 indicates the most extreme difference in importance. The number 0 is used when comparing a criterion to itself, as a score is irrelevant in this instance.

The sum of each row will then be divided by the total sum to get the criteria weight for each criterion.

As you can see, each criterion is only compared to each other once. The score given when comparing one criterion to another must also be recorded as 1 over the value in the mirroring box of the matrix (if 6, then the relation received 1/6).

It is important to remember to only consider by how much is the more valued criterion important. When comparing School to Condition, Condition is a more valued need, therefore, the number needs to show us by how much it is important. It is 9 times more important to have a home in good condition than to be near a good school. In the Condition Row and School Column, the number will read 9. In the School Row, Condition Column, the number will read 1/9

Calculate Row sums and total matrix sum to calculate the weights and the rank

To calculate the criteria weights, we divide each row sum by the total sum of all rows (241.28):

Sum	Pairwise %	Pairwise Rank
57.00	23.6%	1
15.36	6.4%	5
52.17	21.6%	3
3.14	1.3%	10
7.32	3.0%	9
17.51	7.3%	4
11.95	5.0%	7
12.87	5.3%	6
8.95	3.7%	8
55.00	22.8%	2
241.28	100%	

Final List in percentages and in order of high to low criteria.

Criteria	Pairwise %	Pairwise Rank
Price	23.6%	1
Condition	22.8%	2
Safety	21.6%	3
Bedrooms	7.3%	4
School	6.4%	5
Kitchen	5.3%	6
Bathrooms	5.0%	7
Backyard	3.7%	8
Amenities	3.0%	9
Commute	1.3%	10

These percentages represent the relative importance of each criterion in the decision-making process when evaluating and comparing different house options in a suburban neighborhood.

3. Analytic Hierarchy Process (AHP)

This method utilizes the same Comparison chart created for Pairwise. The difference is in the calculation. Rather than dividing the individual score with the total possible score, an average for each input is added and then divided by the total number of entries. This means the score given to Price when compared to School is divided by the total score given to School in that column. This is added to all other comparison scores in the same manner. The total of all entries divided by 10 will give you the AHP weighting percentage. You will notice very minute changes in the weighting, but in some cases, this could be enough to sway the priority order.

Criteria and Pairwise Comparisons

The first step in the AHP process is to identify the criteria or factors important for making the decision. These criteria could be anything from cost and quality to location and reputation. Once the criteria have been established, pairwise comparisons are made between them to determine their relative importance. For example, if we were trying to decide which house to buy, we might compare the importance of location versus size versus price.

Let's say we are trying to decide which house to buy, and we have identified three criteria: location, size, and price. We will make pairwise comparisons between the criteria to determine their relative importance.

	Criteria	Price	School	Safety	Commute	Amenities	Bedrooms	Bathrooms	Kitchen	Backyard	Condition
1	Price	1	8	6	8	8	6	7	6	6	1
2	School	1/8	1	1/8	5	7	1/2	1/2	1/2	1/2	1/9
3	Safety	1/6	8	1	9	9	5	6	6	7	1
4	Commute	1/8	1/5	1/9	1	1/4	1/4	1/3	1/4	1/2	1/8
5	Amenities	1/8	1/7	1/9	4	1	1/3	1/2	1/2	1/2	1/9
6	Bedrooms	1/6	2	1/5	4	3	1	2	3	2	1/7
7	Bathrooms	1/7	2	1/6	3	2	1/2	1	1	2	1/7
8	Kitchen	1/6	2	1/6	4	2	1/3	1	1	2	1/5
9	Backyard	1/6	2	1/7	2	2	1/2	1/2	1/2	1	1/7
10	Condition	1	9	1	8	9	7	7	5	7	1

Normalization of the Comparison Matrix

After the pairwise comparisons have been made, a comparison matrix is created to display the results. This matrix needs to be normalized to ensure that the criteria are comparable. Normalization is done by dividing each element in each column by the sum of the elements in that column. This ensures that the values in each column add up to 1. This creates a matrix of relative importance values.

	Criteria	Price	School	Safety	Commute	Amenities	Bedrooms	Bathrooms	Kitchen	Backyard	Condition
1	Price	0.31	0.23	0.66	0.17	0.18	0.28	0.27	0.25	0.21	0.25
2	School	0.04	0.03	0.01	0.10	0.16	0.02	0.02	0.02	0.02	0.03
3	Safety	0.05	0.23	0.11	0.19	0.21	0.23	0.23	0.25	0.25	0.25
4	Commute	0.04	0.01	0.01	0.02	0.01	0.01	0.01	0.01	0.02	0.03
5	Amenities	0.04	0.00	0.01	0.08	0.02	0.02	0.02	0.02	0.02	0.03
6	Bedrooms	0.05	0.06	0.02	0.08	0.07	0.05	0.08	0.13	0.07	0.04
7	Bathrooms	0.04	0.06	0.02	0.06	0.05	0.02	0.04	0.04	0.07	0.04
8	Kitchen	0.05	0.06	0.02	0.08	0.05	0.02	0.04	0.04	0.07	0.05
9	Backyard	0.05	0.06	0.02	0.04	0.05	0.02	0.02	0.02	0.04	0.04
10	Condition	0.31	0.26	0.11	0.17	0.21	0.33	0.27	0.21	0.25	0.25
	Sum	1.00	1.00	1.00	1.00	1.00	1.00	1.00	1.00	1.00	1.00

Calculation of Relative Weights

With the normalized matrix, we can calculate the relative weight of each criterion. The weight is calculated by taking the arithmetic mean of each matrix row. This gives us a weight for each criterion that reflects its importance relative to the other criteria.

The priority vector is a term used in the Analytic Hierarchy Process (AHP) to refer to a vector of weights or priorities assigned to each criterion or alternative being evaluated. It represents the relative importance of each criterion or alternative in the decision-making process.

In other words, the priority vector is a mathematical representation of the decision maker's preferences or priorities among the criteria or alternatives being evaluated. It provides a way to compare and rank different criteria or alternatives based on their relative importance in the decision-making process.

Criteria	Row Average (AHP %)
Price	0.28
School	0.05
Safety	0.20
Commute	0.02
Amenities	0.03
Bedrooms	0.06
Bathrooms	0.04
Kitchen	0.05
Backyard	0.03
Condition	0.24
Sum	100%

Pairwise Comparisons of Options Against Each Criterion

Once the criteria have been established and their relative importance determined, we can compare options against each criterion. For example, if we were trying to decide which house to buy, we might compare the location, size, and price of House A versus House B. We would use the same pairwise comparison method as before to determine the relative importance of each option.

Calculation of Final Priority Values

Using the weighted sum or weighted product method, we can calculate the final priority value for each option. This gives us an overall score for each option, which we can use to make a decision.

Checking for Consistency

Before making a decision, it's important to check for consistency in the pairwise comparisons. This is done using the consistency ratio, which compares the actual consistency of the pairwise comparisons to the expected consistency. If the consistency ratio is too high, it may be necessary to revise the pairwise comparisons to ensure accuracy.

The consistency ratio is a metric that measures the consistency between pairwise comparisons. For example, suppose we have identified three criteria: taste, price, and availability, and we are comparing apples, oranges, and bananas. We like apples twice as much as oranges (A1/O2 = 2), oranges three times as much as bananas (O2/B3 = 3), and bananas half as much as apples (B3/A1 = 1/2).

To check for consistency, we can calculate the consistency ratio. If the consistency ratio is too high, it indicates an inconsistency in our preferences, and we need to revise the pairwise comparisons or reconsider the criteria we have selected. In this case, the consistency ratio is 0.04, below the threshold of 0.1, indicating that the pairwise comparisons are consistent.

However, if we made a mistake in our comparisons and accidentally rated bananas higher than apples, we would like bananas twice as much as apples (B3/A1 = 2). When we calculate the consistency ratio, it is 0.23, which is above the threshold of 0.1. This indicates an inconsistency in our preferences, and we need to revise the judgments in the matrix or reconsider the criteria we have selected.

To fix the inconsistency, we need to adjust our pairwise comparisons to reflect our true preferences. In this case, we would need to adjust our comparison of apples and bananas to reflect that we like apples more than bananas. We might rate apples twice as much as bananas (A1/B3 = 2) instead of bananas twice as much as apples. This would result in a consistency ratio of 0.06, which is still below the threshold of 0.1 and indicates that our pairwise comparisons are consistent.

In summary, the consistency ratio is an important metric for ensuring the accuracy and reliability of our decisions. By checking for consistency and adjusting our pairwise comparisons as needed, we can make informed decisions with confidence.

To calculate the consistency ratio:

Step 1: Calculate the weighted sum of each column of the comparison matrix.

We then divide each element in the matrix by its corresponding column sum and take the average of each row. This gives us the row average, which measures how consistent the pairwise comparisons are.

Weighted Sum
1.24320
1.92162
1.41061
1.50295
1.97477
1.50443
1.57334
1.66082
1.57210
1.33961

Step 2: Calculate the principal eigenvalue. The principal eigenvalue is the sum of the product of each matrix element with its corresponding criteria weight in the priority vector. To calculate the principal eigenvalue, multiply each element of the normalized matrix by its corresponding weight in the priority vector and then sum the resulting products.

Step 3: Divide each row sum by the weight of the criterion from the priority vector

Principle Eigen Value
11.25319

Step 4: Calculate the consistency index (CI) The consistency index (CI) is a measure of how consistent the AHP matrix is. It is calculated by subtracting the number of criteria from the principal eigenvalue and then dividing the result by the number of criteria minus one. The formula for the consistency index is:

$$CI = (\lambda max - n) / (n - 1)$$

$$(11.25319 - 10) / (10 - 1)$$

where λmax is the principal eigenvalue and n is the number of criteria.

CI

0.13924

Step 5: Calculate the random index (RI). The random index (RI) is a reference value that is used to evaluate the consistency of the AHP matrix. It is based on the number of criteria and is found in a table that is based on the number of criteria in the AHP matrix. For example, for a 10x10 matrix, the RI is 1.49.

Step 6: Calculate the consistency ratio (CR). The consistency ratio (CR) is the ratio of the consistency index to the random index. The formula for the consistency ratio is:

CR = CI / RI

0.13924 / 1.49

CR

0.09345

Step 7: Interpret the results. If the consistency ratio is less than or equal to 0.1, the AHP matrix is considered to be consistent. If the consistency ratio is greater than 0.1, the AHP matrix is considered to be inconsistent, and you may need to revise your judgments in the matrix or reconsider the criteria you have selected.

Calculation Methods in AHP

There are several methods for calculating the weights in AHP, including the Approximate Eigen Vector method, Largest Eigenvector method, Geometric Mean method, and Fuzzy Geometric Mean method. These methods differ in the way they calculate the weights, but they all follow the same basic process.

Applications of AHP

AHP has been applied in a wide variety of fields, including business, engineering, environmental science, and health care. In business, AHP has been used to make decisions on product development, marketing strategy, and investment decisions. In engineering, AHP has been used to evaluate design options and select suppliers. In environmental science, AHP has been used to assess the impacts of land use change and prioritize conservation efforts. AHP has been used in health care to evaluate treatment options and allocate resources.

Conclusion

In conclusion, AHP is a powerful decision-making method that can help to simplify complex decisions by breaking them down into smaller, more manageable steps. By identifying criteria, making pairwise comparisons, normalizing matrices, and calculating weights and final priorities, AHP can provide a structured approach to decision-making that can help ensure accuracy and consistency. With its wide range of applications and potential for further research, AHP is a valuable tool for anyone facing difficult decisions.

References

Saaty, T. L. (2008). Decision making with the analytic hierarchy process. *International journal of services sciences*, 1(1), 83-98.

Kumar, A., & Sharma, R. K. (2015). Application of the AHP method for selection of supplier in a manufacturing organization. International Journal of Quality & Reliability Management, 32(6), 688-701.

Almeida-Dias, J., & Soares, C. G. (2015). Multi-criteria decision analysis for strategic environmental assessment of land use plans: A case study in Portugal. Journal of environmental management, 154, 48-57.

Moshagen, M. (2013). Multi-criteria decision making in health care. Zeitschrift für Psychologie, 221(4), 225-238.

4. Ben Franklin method (Pros and Cons)

is a simple decision-making technique that involves listing the pros and cons of each alternative and comparing them to determine the best choice. Here's an example of how you can use the Ben Franklin method to decide which house to buy:

Step 1: Define the Alternatives The first step is to define the alternatives, which are the different houses that you are considering purchasing. Let's say you are considering two houses: House A and House B.

Step 2: List the Pros and Cons The next step is to list the pros and cons of each alternative. You can do this by creating a table with two columns, one for pros and one for cons, for each house.

House A:

Pros	Cons
Large backyard	Expensive
Modern appliances	Far from work
Great school district	Needs repairs
Plenty of natural light	Few amenities

House B:

Pros	Cons
Close to work	Small backyard
Affordable	Older appliances
Recently renovated	Okay school district
Access to amenities	Limited natural light

Step 3: Assign Weights to the Pros and Cons The next step is to assign weights to the pros and cons to reflect their relative importance. For example, if you value having a large backyard more than having modern appliances, you can assign a higher weight to the large backyard pro. You can assign weights on a scale of 1 to 10, with 10 being the most important.

House A:

Pros	Cons
Large backyard (9)	Expensive (10)
Modern appliances (5)	Far from work (8)
Great school district (8)	Needs repairs (7)
Plenty of natural light (6)	Few amenities (4)

House B:

Pros	Cons
Close to work (10)	Small backyard (5)
Affordable (8)	Older appliances (6)
Recently renovated (7)	Okay school district (5)
Access to amenities (9)	Limited natural light (4)

Step 4: Total the Scores The next step is to total the scores for each alternative by subtracting the total cons score from the total pros score for each house.

House A:
(Total Pros Score = 28, Total Cons Score = 29) Total Score = 28 - 29 = -1

House B:
(Total Pros Score = 34, Total Cons Score = 20) Total Score =
34 - 20 = 14

Step 5: Compare the Results The final step is to compare the
results and choose the alternative with the higher score. In this
example, House B has a higher score of 14, which means that it
is the best choice according to the Ben Franklin method.

5. Six Thinking Hats

Step 1: Define the Alternatives. Let's say you are considering
two houses, House A and House B.

Step 2: Identify the Hats Next, look at the decision from six
different perspectives or "hats":

- White Hat: Consider the information you have about
  each house, such as its location, size, and price.
- Red Hat: Consider your emotional response to each
  house, such as how you feel when you're inside each
  house.
- Black Hat: Consider the potential downsides or
  negative aspects of each house.
- Yellow Hat: Consider the potential upsides or positive
  aspects of each house.
- Green Hat: Consider creative or innovative ideas for
  each house, such as ways you could renovate or
  personalize the space.
- Blue Hat: Consider the big picture and how each house
  fits into your long-term goals.

Step 3: Evaluate Each House: Evaluate each house based on each hat:

House	White Hat	Red Hat	Black Hat	Yellow Hat	Green Hat	Blue Hat
A	Located in a quiet neighborhood	Feels cozy and comfortable	Needs some repairs and updates	Has a big backyard with a pool	Could add a home theater in the basement	Fits within the budget and is close to work
B	Located in a busy area with lots of amenities	Feels spacious and open	Needs some minor repairs	Has a modern kitchen with high-end appliances	Could add a gym in the spare room	Is larger and has more rooms for a growing family

Step 4: Analyze the Hats: Analyze the information for each hat and determine which house is the best option:

- White Hat: House A is in a quiet neighborhood, and House B is in a busy area with many amenities. It depends on your preference for location.
- Red Hat: You feel cozy and comfortable in House A and spacious and open in House B. It depends on your personal preference and lifestyle.
- Black Hat: House A needs some repairs and updates, while House B needs minor repairs. Both require some investment.
- Yellow Hat: House A has a big backyard with a pool, while House B has a modern kitchen with high-end appliances. It depends on what amenities are more important to you.
- Green Hat: House A could add a home theater in the basement, while House B could add a gym in the spare room. Both have the potential for improvement.
- Blue Hat: House A fits within the budget and is close to work, while House B is larger and has more room for a growing family. It depends on your long-term goals and plans.

Step 5: Evaluate the Overall Picture Evaluate the overall picture and weigh the information from each hat to make a decision. For this example, it depends on your personal preferences and goals.

6. SWOT Analysis

Step 1: Define Your Options.

Step 2: List the Strengths, Weaknesses, Opportunities, and Threats. List out the strengths, weaknesses, opportunities, and threats for each house:

House	Strengths	Weaknesses	Opportunities	Threats
A	Located in a quiet neighborhood	Needs some repairs and updates	Has a big backyard with a pool that can be renovated	The repairs and updates may be costly
B	Fits within the budget and is close to work	Limited back yard	Can add a home theater in the basement	May not have enough space for a growing family
C	Located in a busy area with lots of amenities	Needs some minor repairs	Is larger and has more rooms for a growing family	May be more expensive and have higher property taxes
D	Has a modern kitchen with high-end appliances	May not have a big backyard or pool	Can add a gym in the spare room	Crowded neighborhood

Step 3: Analyze the SWOTs. Analyze each house's strengths, weaknesses, opportunities, and threats and determine which house has the most advantages or disadvantages. For this example, it depends on your priorities and trade-offs.

260 The Decision Principles

7. Cost-Benefit Analysis

Step 1: Identify the costs and benefits of each alternative. For example, Alternative A costs $250,000 and has a large backyard, while Alternative B costs $225,000 and has a pool.

Step 2: Evaluate the costs and benefits. For Alternative A, the benefit of the large backyard is weighed against the higher cost. For Alternative B, the benefit of the pool is weighed against the lower cost.

Step 3: Compare the costs and benefits. Calculate the ratio of benefits to costs for each alternative. For example, if Alternative A has $100,000 in benefits and $250,000 in costs, the ratio is 0.4. If Alternative B has $80,000 in benefits and $225,000 in costs, the ratio is 0.36.

Step 4: Choose the alternative with the highest ratio. In this case, Alternative A has a higher ratio, so it is the better option.

8. Game Theory

Step 1: Analyze the decisions of other parties. For example, if you are bidding on a house in a competitive market, research the behavior of other bidders.

Step 2: Identify the potential outcomes. Determine the range of potential outcomes and the likelihood of each.

Step 3: Choose the optimal strategy. Based on the potential outcomes and the actions of other bidders, develop the optimal bidding strategy.

9. Pareto Analysis

Step 1: Identify the criteria. For example, location, price, size, and amenities.

Step 2: Rank the criteria. Determine the importance of each criterion. For example, location is most important, followed by price, size, and then amenities.

Step 3: Evaluate the alternatives. For each alternative, evaluate how well it performs on each criterion.

Step 4: Choose the alternative that performs the best on the most important criteria. For example, if House A has the best location and price, while House B has the best size and amenities, House A may be the better choice.

Appendix II

The Cognitive Bias Wheel

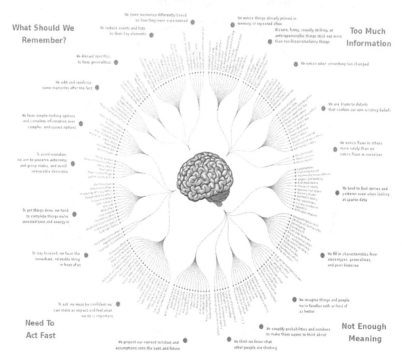

Source: This file was derived from: The Cognitive Bias Codex - 180+ biases, designed by John Manoogian III (jm3).png

Biases About Too Much Information

Includes biases related to the overwhelming amount of information that we encounter in our daily lives.

Anchoring Bias

The tendency to rely too heavily on the first piece of information encountered when making decisions. For example, a negotiator may be anchored to the initial offer made by the other party, even if it is unreasonable.

Availability Heuristic

The tendency to rely on easily recalled examples or instances when making judgments or decisions. For example, a person may believe that flying is more dangerous than driving because plane crashes are often reported in the news, even though driving accidents are more common.

Base Rate Fallacy

The tendency to ignore general information about probabilities when making specific judgments. For example, someone might overestimate the chance of winning the lottery because they focus on stories of winners rather than the low odds.

Blind Spot Bias

The tendency to see oneself as less biased than others or to overlook one's own biases. For example, someone might believe that they are objective in a political debate while accusing their opponent of being biased.

Confirmation Bias

The tendency to seek out and focus on information that confirms our existing beliefs while ignoring or dismissing contradictory evidence. For example, a person who believes in a particular conspiracy theory may only read sources that support their view and reject those that don't.

Choice-Supportive Bias

The tendency to remember one's choices as being better than they actually were. For example, someone might believe that the car they bought was the best option, even if it had problems.

Framing Effect

The tendency to be influenced by the way information is presented, such as the order or wording of options. For example, a person may be more likely to choose an option that is presented as a gain (such as "you will gain $100") rather than as a loss (such as "you will lose $100").

Frequency Illusion

The tendency to notice things more often after first being exposed to them. For example, after buying a new car, you notice the same model more often on the road.

Negativity Bias

The tendency to give more weight and attention to negative experiences or information than to positive ones. For example, a person may remember criticism from a boss more vividly than praise for a job well done.

Ostrich Effect

The tendency to avoid information or situations that are perceived as unpleasant or threatening. For example, someone might ignore a health problem because they fear the diagnosis.

Biases Where You Need to Act Fast

Includes biases related to the pressure to make quick decisions.

Belief Bias

The tendency to judge the strength of arguments based on how believable the conclusion is rather than on the quality of the evidence. For example, someone might reject a scientifically-supported idea because it goes against their beliefs.

Conjunction Fallacy

The tendency to judge the conjunction of two events as more likely than one of the events alone. For example, someone might think it is more likely that a person is both a doctor and a musician than just a doctor.

False Consensus Effect

The tendency to overestimate how much other people share our beliefs or attitudes. For example, someone might assume that most people agree with their political views, even if that is not true.

Fundamental Attribution Error

The tendency to overemphasize personality traits and underemphasize situational factors when explaining the behavior of others. For example, a person may assume that someone late for a meeting is always tardy rather than considering the possibility that they were delayed by traffic or an unexpected event.

Illusion of Control

The tendency to overestimate our control over events. For example, a person might believe they have control over the outcome of a coin toss.

Illusory Superiority

The tendency for people to overestimate their own abilities or qualities in relation to others. For example, someone might think they are a better driver than most other people.

Overconfidence Bias

The tendency to be overly confident in one's judgments or abilities. For example, a person may believe they can successfully navigate a dangerous mountain trail even though they have no experience in hiking or mountaineering.

Self-Serving Bias

The tendency to attribute one's successes to internal factors (such as ability or effort) and one's failures to external factors (such as bad luck or unfair circumstances). For example, a student may attribute a good grade on an exam to their intelligence and hard work while blaming a poor grade on the difficulty of the questions.

Status Quo Bias

The tendency to prefer things to stay the same rather than making a change. For example, a person may choose to stick with a current healthcare plan, even if a different plan would provide better coverage at a lower cost.

Sunk Cost Fallacy

The tendency to continue investing in a project or decision, even when it no longer makes logical sense. For example, a business may continue investing in a product that is no longer profitable simply because they have already invested a large amount of money in it.

Biases About Not Enough Meaning

Includes biases related to our need to make sense of the world around us.

Authority Bias

The tendency to attribute greater accuracy to the opinion or action of an authority figure. For example, someone might trust a doctor's medical advice more than a person with no medical training.

Gambler's Fallacy

The belief is that past events affect the probability of future events in independent trials. So, for example, someone might think that a roulette wheel is more likely to land on red after several spins of black.

Halo Effect

The tendency to form a general impression of a person based on a single trait or characteristic. For example, a physically attractive person may be perceived as kinder, more intelligent, or more competent than someone less attractive.

Hindsight Bias

The tendency to see events as more predictable than they are after they have occurred. For example, someone might say, "I knew that would happen" after a surprising event, even if they didn't really predict it.

In-group Bias

The tendency to favor one's own group over other groups. For example, someone might feel more comfortable around people from their own culture or religion.

Normalcy Bias

The tendency to underestimate the likelihood of a disaster or crisis occurring and the potential impact of such an event. For example, someone might not prepare for a hurricane because they don't think it will be as bad as predicted.

Outcome Bias

The tendency to judge the quality of a decision based on its outcome, rather than on the quality of the decision-making process. For example, someone might think a decision was good if it led to a positive outcome, even if it was based on flawed reasoning.

Pro-innovation Bias

The tendency to overvalue new and innovative ideas, and undervalue traditional or established ones. For example, a company might invest in a new technology even if it is not proven to be effective simply because it is new and innovative.

Recency Bias

The tendency is to give more weight to recent events or experiences than past ones. For example, someone might judge a company's performance based on its recent quarterly earnings, even if it has a long history of success.

Rosy Retrospection

The tendency to remember past events in a more positive light than they were. For example, remembering high school as a great time, even if there were many difficulties and challenges.

Biases About What Should We Remember
Includes biases related to our memory and recall.

Absent-mindedness
The tendency to forget things or overlook details due to lack of attention. For example, people might forget their keys or phone because they were distracted when putting them down.

Cryptomnesia
The phenomenon where a person thinks they have come up with a new idea, but it is something they have heard or seen before and forgotten. For example, a musician might accidentally plagiarize a song they heard years ago and forgot about.

False Memory
The phenomenon where a person remembers an event that did not occur or remembers an event differently than it actually happened. For example, someone might believe they were at a concert they never actually attended.

Fading Affect Bias
The tendency to remember positive events with stronger emotional intensity than negative events as time passes, for example, remembering a great vacation but forgetting the minor inconveniences during the trip.

Misattribution of Memory
The phenomenon where a person remembers something accurately but attributes it to the wrong source. For example, a person might remember hearing a news story from a trusted source but actually heard it from a less reliable source.

Negativity Bias

The tendency to focus more on negative information than positive information. For example, remembering the one bad review of a restaurant instead of the many good ones.

Recency Bias

The tendency to give more weight to recent events or information than to older events or information. For example, a hiring manager may be more impressed by a job candidate's most recent work experience, even if it is less relevant to the position than their earlier experience.

Serial Position Effect

The tendency to remember the first and last items on a list more easily than the items in the middle. For example, remembering the first and last items on a grocery list but forgetting some items in the middle.

Source Confusion

The phenomenon where a person remembers information accurately but confuses the source of the information. For example, a person might remember hearing about a news story but not remember if they heard it from a friend or read it in the newspaper.

Testing Effect

The phenomenon where practicing recalling information (e.g., taking practice tests) can improve long-term memory retention. For example, a student might improve their test scores by taking practice quizzes on the material.

Appendix III

Fast Decisions

1. Choosing which item to grab from a falling shelf
2. Deciding to grab onto something stable when you lose your balance
3. Pulling your hand away from a hot stove or other sources of heat
4. Deciding to move out of the way of a fast-moving bicycle on the sidewalk
5. Choosing to stop and help someone who is injured or in danger
6. Deciding to speak up when you witness something morally wrong
7. Reacting quickly to avoid danger or harm
8. Making snap decisions, such as in emergency situations
9. Making a split-second decision in a game or competition
10. Quickly responding to a customer complaint or issue
11. Choosing to go with your first instinct during a job interview
12. Swerving your car when another driver suddenly veers into your lane
13. Deciding to trust your intuition when time-sensitive
14. Deciding to rely on your prior experience when making a quick decision
15. Choosing to give someone the benefit of the doubt and assume positive intentions, even if you don't fully understand their actions

Slow Decisions

1. Deciding on a career path or job change
2. Buying a house or property
3. Choosing a life partner or getting married
4. Starting a family or having children
5. Making a significant investment
6. Choosing a graduate school or degree program
7. Relocating to a new city or country
8. Making a major business decision
9. Deciding whether to end a long-term relationship
10. Deciding to undergo a significant medical procedure or treatment
11. Deciding to change careers or industries
12. Moving to a new city or country
13. Deciding whether to start your own business or work for someone else
14. Choosing a retirement plan or investment strategy
15. Making a decision about a legal matter, such as a lawsuit or contract

Appendix IV

Popular Life Decisions

Decision	Ramifications	Proposed Criteria
Deciding on travel destination and itinerary	BAD = no fun, bad experience, wasted money and time GOOD = amazing memories, great weather, good experience	1. Budget 2. Safety 3. Accessibility 4. Climate 5. Cultural Attractions 6. Natural Attractions 7. Accommodation options 8. Food and Drink Options 9. Language Barriers 10. Travel Style
Deciding on a college major or course of study	BAD = lack of interest, dropout, fail GOOD = sustainable motivation and interest, successful career, passion	1. Personal Interests 2. Career Prospects 3. Academic Strengths 4. Financial Considerations 5. Location and Accessibility 6. Faculty and Resources 7. Reputation and Accreditation 8. Return on Investment 9. Flexibility and Adaptability 10. Market Demand
Choosing where to live	BAD = unhappiness, unsafe, lack of community and companionship GOOD = community, close to amenities, ease of life	1. Cost of Living 2. Safety 3. Proximity to Work or School 4. Access to Amenities 5. Quality of Schools 6. Climate 7. Cultural and Recreational Opportunities 8. Community and Social Life 9. Public Transportation 10. Environmental Factors

Decision	Ramifications	Proposed Criteria
Choosing a life partner	BAD = divorce, financial loss, messy and angry relationship GOOD = fulfillment, happiness, loving partnership	1. Compatibility 2. Communication 3. Trust 4. Emotional intelligence 5. Shared goals 6. Respect 7. Support 8. Chemistry 9. Financial stability 10. Family values
Making health and wellness decisions	BAD = death, disease, poor quality of life GOOD = vitality, agility, active lifestyle	1. Effectiveness 2. Safety 3. Affordability 4. Accessibility 5. Convenience 6. Sustainability 7. Personal preferences 8. Expert recommendations 9. Evidence-based 10. Potential for Harm
Choosing to volunteer or donate to charities	BAD = waste time or money GOOD = make a significant impact for good	1. Impact 2. Alignment 3. Transparency 4. Time Commitment 5. Skills and Expertise 6. Reputation 7. Accessibility 8. Personal Capacity 9. Geographic Scope 10. Long-term Partnership
Deciding on long-term goals and aspirations	BAD = no growth, spending time and energy on low-priority items GOOD = fulfillment and growth, accomplishment, and achievement	1. Relevance 2. Feasibility 3. Impact 4. Timeframe 5. Cost 6. Risk 7. Flexibility 8. Passion 9. Skills and Abilities 10. Market Trends

Decision	Ramifications	Proposed Criteria
Deciding on a healthcare provider or specialist	BAD = poor medical advice or treatment GOOD = improved health and vitality	1. Qualifications and Credentials 2. Experience 3. Reputation 4. Availability 5. Location 6. Insurance Coverage 7. Communication Skills 8. Treatment Approach 9. Patient-Centered Care 10. Follow-up Care
Making decisions about saving and investing money	BAD = loss of capital and financial security GOOD = strong returns, financial freedom	1. Return on Investment 2. Risk Tolerance 3. Liquidity 4. Diversification 5. Fees and Expenses 6. Time Horizon 7. Tax Implications 8. Time Horizon 9. Investment Goals 10. Diversification
Choosing to make a major purchase, such as a car or home	BAD = depreciates in value, financial burden GOOD = improve quality of life, enjoyment	1. Price 2. Quality 3. Features 4. Safety 5. Maintenance 6. Resale Value 7. Warranty 8. Fuel Efficiency 9. Location 10. Size

Popular Career Decisions

Decision	Ramifications	Proposed Criteria
Deciding on a career path	BAD = unhappiness, decreased motivation, unfulfillment GOOD = fulfilling career, increased energy, passion	1. Personal Interests 2. Job Satisfaction 3. Salary and Benefits 4. Education and Training 5. Job Market 6. Work Environment 7. Personal Values
Deciding whether to switch industries or stay in the same field	BAD = failure, shame/embarrassment, loss of income GOOD = increased motivation, excitement, learning, growth	1. Job Satisfaction 2. Skills and Experience 3. Industry Growth 4. Personal Goals 5. Networking Opportunities 6. Geographic Location 7. Company Culture 8. Risk Tolerance
Deciding whether to pursue a leadership role or stay in a non-managerial position	BAD = boredom, in over your head, loss of opportunity GOOD = fulfillment, more money, challenging in a good way	1. Career Goals 2. Skills and Experience 3. Work-Life Balance 4. Compensation and Benefits: 5. Personal Growth and Development 6. Organizational Culture 7. Job Security 8. Impact on Others

Decision	Ramifications	Proposed Criteria
Choosing to leave a current job or company for another opportunity	BAD = loss of seniority/tenure, difficult transition, less freed GOOD = improved culture, renewed motivation, growth, new opportunities	1. Compensation 2. Career Growth 3. Company Culture 4. Commute 5. Work-Life Balance 6. Job Security 7. Reputation 8. Job Responsibilities 9. Team and Management: 10. Personal Goals
Deciding between multiple job offers	BAD = misalignment of culture, less pay, inflexible hours GOOD = more money, friendly colleagues, enjoyment	1. Job responsibilities and duties: 2. Salary and benefits 3. Company culture 4. Career growth opportunities: 5. Work-life balance 6. Reputation and industry standing 7. Location and commute. 8. Company size and structure: 9. Company mission and values 10. Employee satisfaction and retention
Choosing a course for continued education or training	BAD = wasted time, wasted money, useless information GOOD = improved credentials, intelligence, and experience, more opportunities	1. Cost 2. Time commitment 3. Career prospects 4. Flexibility 5. Reputation 6. Support services 7. Personal goals. 8. Return on investment 9. Location 10. Admission requirements

Decision	Ramifications	Proposed Criteria
Whether to start your own business or work for someone else	BAD = loss of income, no free time, stress GOOD = freedom, flexible schedule, income	1. Risk Tolerance 2. Autonomy 3. Passion 4. Work-Life Balance 5. Skillset 6. Growth Potential 7. Work Environment 8. Personal Goals 9. Resources
Choosing to continue education with post-graduate studies or professional development courses	BAD = wasted time, wasted money, useless information GOOD = improved credentials, intelligence, and experience, more opportunities	1. Relevance 2. Cost 3. Time commitment 4. Reputation 5. Networking opportunities 6. Flexibility 7. Career advancement 8. Learning environment
Evaluating multiple companies to see which is the best fit	BAD = unhappiness, decreased motivation, unfulfillment GOOD = fulfilling career, increased energy, passion	1. Experience 2. Availability 3. Compatibility 4. Reputation 5. Resources 6. Cost 7. Feedback

Popular Business Decisions

Decision	Ramifications	Proposed Criteria
Choosing a project management tool or software	BAD = unfinished projects, incompatible systems, disorganization GOOD = improved time management, better collaboration, completed projects	1. Features 2. Ease of use 3. Scalability 4. Integration 5. Security 6. Cost 7. Customization 8. Customer support 9. Mobile accessibility 10. Training resources
Making decisions about social media use, including the frequency and types of posts	BAD = wasted time, insufficient activity/likes, ineffective content GOOD = good engagement, heightened exposure, community building	1. Relevance 2. Audience 3. Engagement 4. Timing 5. Consistency 6. Creativity 7. Metrics 8. Reputation 9. Legal and ethical considerations 10. Cost
Deciding on a candidate to hire for a specific role	BAD = wasted resources, wrong hire, incompatibility GOOD = team synergy, increased productivity, successful business	1. Compensation 2. Job responsibilities 3. Company culture 4. Career growth opportunities 5. Work-life balance 6. Location 7. Reputation 8. Job security 9. Company size 10. Personal values

Decision	Ramifications	Proposed Criteria
Deciding on the values and culture that the organization wants to promote and instill in its employees	BAD = misalignment, confusion, lack of focus on overall company goals GOOD = clarity, understanding, team unity	1. Alignment with goals and objectives 2. Engagement and satisfaction 3. Ethical and responsible behavior 4. Innovation and creativity 5. Customer satisfaction and loyalty 6. Consistency 7. Diversity and inclusion 8. Flexibility and adaptability 9. Leadership behavior 10. Continuous improvement
Deciding who will take over leadership roles in the organization in the event of retirement, promotion, or unexpected departures	BAD = decreased morale, disrupted team dynamics, loss of time and money GOOD = innovation/creativity, motivation/excitement, team building	1. Leadership potential 2. Organizational fit 3. Succession planning 4. Development 5. Diversity and inclusion 6. Performance management 7. Risk management. 8. Knowledge management 9. Succession 10. Feedback and evaluation
Implementing a wellness program for employees	BAD = high turnover, sick days, burnout GOOD = happy employees, better mental health, more invested employees	1. Employee Needs 2. Budget 3. Wellness Goals 4. Program Design 5. Participation 6. Communication 7. Data Collection 8. Accessibility 9. Resources 10. Evaluation

Decision	Ramifications	Proposed Criteria
Which firms to invest in based on business and financial risk	BAD = lost money, ruined reputation, loss of future opportunities GOOD = make money, create connections, expand business	1. Financial viability 2. Strategic alignment 3. Market position 4. Synergies 5. Operational considerations 6. Human resources 7. Intellectual property 8. Regulatory and legal considerations 9. Integration 10. Cultural fit
What product to launch	BAD = legal implications, financial loss, shame/embarrassment GOOD = effective due diligence process, successful acquisition, expanded business	1. Compliance with regulations: 2. Litigation history 3. Intellectual property 4. Antitrust concerns 5. Employment law 6. Environmental regulations 7. Tax liabilities 8. Due diligence 9. Insurance coverage 10. Exit strategies
What business functions to outsource	BAD = poor quality work, mismanaged projects, high costs GOOD = improved productivity, more internal resources for high-impact and creative endeavors, saving money	1. Cost savings 2. Expertise and specialization 3. Quality of service 4. Potential risks 5. Contract terms and conditions 6. Compatibility with company culture 7. Geographic location 8. Communication and collaboration 9. Transition plan 10. Performance monitoring

Bibliography

Krockow, E.M. (2018, September 27). How many decisions do we make each day? *Psychology Today.* https://www.psychologytoday.com/us/blog/stretching-theory/201809/how-many-decisions-do-we-make-each-day

Project Management Institute. (2018). Pulse of the Profession. https://www.pmi.org/learning/thought-leadership/pulse/pulse-of-the-profession-2018

O'Sullivan, E. D., & Schofield, S. J. (2018). Cognitive bias in clinical medicine. *The journal of the Royal College of Physicians of Edinburgh, 48*(3), 225–232.

Johnson, D., Fowler, J. (2011). The evolution of overconfidence. *Nature* 477, 317–320.

Nisbett RE, Wilson TD. (1977). Telling more than we can know: Verbal reports on mental process. Psychological Review, 84, 231–259. https://doi.org/10.1037/0033-295X.84.3.231

Bessey D. (2021). Loss Aversion and Health Behaviors: Results from Two Incentivized Economic Experiments. *Healthcare (Basel), 9*(8), 1040.

Halvorson, H. G. (2022, December 16). How to Recognize Negative Thought Loops and Stop Obsessing. Psychology Today. https://www.psychologytoday.com/us/blog/the-stories-we-tell/202212/how-to-recognize-negative-thought-loops-and-stop-obsessing

284 The Decision Principles

Kahneman, D. (2011). *Thinking, Fast and Slow*. Farrar, Straus and Giroux.

While the terms "System 1" and "System 2" in Kahneman's model primarily refer to two modes of thinking related to *cognitive processes*, it is also important to note that there are many bodily processes that occur *unconsciously*, such as the beating of our hearts and the regulation of blood flow. These bodily processes are typically controlled by the autonomic nervous system, which is responsible for regulating many involuntary bodily functions. It is important to note that these types of decisions are different from the types of decisions that are made through *cognitive processes*, as they are not typically subject to conscious thought or decision-making.

Frankl, V. E. (2006). Man's Search for Meaning: An Introduction to Logotherapy. Beacon Press.

Shapiro, S., Jazaieri, H., & Goldin, P. (2012) Mindfulness-based stress reduction effects on moral reasoning and decision making. The Journal of Positive Psychology 7(6), 504-515

Ibid.

Gladwell, M. (2007). *Blink: The Power of Thinking Without Thinking*. Back Bay Books.

Alliance for Decision Education. A wonderful organization co-founded by Annie that empowers students with essential skills and dispositions for making better decisions.

American Psychological Association. (2015). *Stress in America: Paying with our health*. http://www.apa.org/news/press/releases/stress/2014/stress-report.pdf.

Lerner, J. S., Li, Y., Valdesolo, P., & Kassam, K. S. (2015). Emotion and decision making. *Annual Review of Psychology*, 66, 799-823.

Isen, A. M., & Patrick, R. (1983). The effect of positive feelings on risk-taking: When the chips are down. *Organizational Behavior and Human Performance*, 31*(2)*, 194-202.

Dweck C. S. (2006). *Mindset: The new psychology of success.* Random House.

Roseman, I. J. (1984). Cognitive determinants of emotion: A structural theory. In K. R. Scherer & P. Ekman (Eds.), *Approaches to emotion* (pp. 145-166). Erlbaum.

Lazarus, R. S. (1991). Emotion and Adaptation. New York: Oxford University Press

Damasio, A. R. (1994). Descartes' error and the future of human life. *Scientific American*, 271*(4)*, 144-147.

Wood, W., Neal, D. T., & Quinn, J. M. (2019). Habits in everyday life: Thought, emotion, and action. *Journal of Personality and Social Psychology*, 117*(6)*, 1110–1129.

The Power of Habit: Why We Do What We Do in Life and Business by Charles Duhigg was published by Random House in 2012.

"Limitless" is a 2011 American science fiction thriller film directed by Neil Burger and starring Bradley Cooper, Robert De Niro, and Abbie Cornish.

Robbins, M. (2017). The 5 Second Rule: Transform Your Life, Work, and Confidence with Everyday Courage. Savio Republic.

Crowe, C. (Director). (1996). Jerry Maguire [Motion picture]. United States: TriStar Pictures.

Svenson, O., & Maule, A. J. (Eds.) (1993). *Time pressure and stress in human judgment and decision making.* Plenum.

Vasilescu, C. (2011). Effective strategic decision making. *Journal of Defense Resources Management (JoDRM), 2(1),* 101-106.

Saaty, T. L. (1980). The Analytic Hierarchy Process: Planning, Priority Setting, Resource Allocation. New York: McGraw-Hill.

Sackett, P. R., Lievens, F., & Van Iddekinge, C. H. (2021). Using situational judgment tests to increase diversity in applicant pools: Evidence from a large-scale field experiment. Journal of Applied Psychology, 106(1), 61–81. https://doi.org/10.1037/apl0000518

Dane, E., & Pratt, M. G. (2007). Exploring intuition and its role in managerial decision making. Academy of Management Journal, 50(1), 1-13. https://doi.org/10.5465/amj.2007.24160888

Festinger, L., & Carlsmith, J. M. (1959). Cognitive consequences of forced compliance. The Journal of Abnormal and Social Psychology, 58(2), 203-210.

Dane, E., & Pratt, M. G. (2007). Exploring intuition and its role in managerial decision making. Journal of Behavioral Decision Making, 20(1), 1-21. doi:10.1002/bdm.544

Source: "The Power of Intuition in Decision Making" by Gary Klein, *Harvard Business Review,* June 2003.

Source: Vance, A. (2015). Elon Musk: Tesla, SpaceX, and the quest for a fantastic future. HarperCollins.

Darwin, C. (1859). On the Origin of Species by Means of Natural Selection, or the Preservation of Favoured Races in the Struggle for Life. John Murray.

Gomez L. E. & Bernet P. (n.d.). Diversity improves performance and outcomes. *Journal of the National Medical Association* (383–392). https://doi.org/10.1016/j.jnma.2019.01.006

Duhigg, C. (2012). The Power of Habit: Why We Do What We Do in Life and Business. Random House.

Thaler, R. H., & Sunstein, C. R. (2008). *Nudge: Improving decisions about health, wealth, and happiness.* Penguin.

Killgore, W. D., Balkin, T. J., & Wesensten, N. J. (2017). Impaired decision making following 49 h of sleep deprivation. Sleep, 40(5), zsx056.

Rasch, B., Büchel, C., Gais, S., & Born, J. (2019). Odor cues during slow-wave sleep prompt declarative memory consolidation. Nature Communications, 10(1), 1-11.

Yoo, S. S., Gujar, N., Hu, P., Jolesz, F. A., & Walker, M. P. (2007). The human emotional brain without sleep--a prefrontal amygdala disconnect. Current Biology, 17(20), R877-8. doi: 10.1016/j.cub.2007.08.007

Goldstein-Piekarski, A. N., Greer, S. M., Saletin, J. M., & Walker, M. P. (2015). Sleep deprivation impairs the human central and peripheral nervous system discrimination of social threat. Journal of Neuroscience, 35(28), 10135-10145.

Source: Isaacson, W. (2011). Steve Jobs. Simon & Schuster.

Robins, L. N., Davis, D. H., & Nurco, D. N. (1974). How permanent was Vietnam drug addiction? American Journal of Public Health, 64(12 Suppl), 38–43.

This can be a frustrating and unproductive state to be in, as it can lead to missed opportunities, wasted time and resources, and increased stress and anxiety. Analysis paralysis can also cause decision-makers to lose confidence in their abilities, leading to a further delay in making a decision.

Bezos, J. (2016). 2016 Letter to Amazon Shareholders. Amazon.com, Inc. Retrieved from https://www.aboutamazon.com/news/company-news/2016-letter-to-shareholders

Asana. (2022). *Anatomy of Work Global Index 2022.* *https://investors.asana.com/news/news-details/2022/Asana-Anatomy-of-Work-Index-2022-Work-About-Work-Hampering-Organizational-Agility/default.aspx*

Pignatiello, G. A., Tsivitse, E., O'Brien, J., Kraus, N., & Hickman, R. L., Jr (2022). Decision fatigue among clinical nurses during the COVID-19 pandemic. *Journal of clinical nursing, 31 (7-8),* 869–877.

Made in the USA
Middletown, DE
20 October 2023

41131998R00166